HAND *and* HOME

HAND and HOME
The Homes of American Craftsmen

Text by TOMMY SIMPSON, with LISA HAMMEL

Photographs by WILLIAM BENNETT SEITZ

Foreword by LISA HAMMEL

A Bulfinch Press Book   Little, Brown and Company   Boston   New York   London

First Paperback Edition, 1998

Library of Congress Cataloging-in-Publication Data

Simpson, Tommy
    Hand and home: inside the homes of American craftsmen/
Tommy Simpson; photographs by William Bennett Seitz; foreword by
Lisa Hammel.—1st ed.
        p.   cm.
    "A Bulfinch Press Book."
    ISBN 8-8212-2051-9 (HC)
    ISBN 0-8212-2568-5 (PB)
    1. Artisans—Homes and haunts—United States. 2. Interior
decoration—United States—History—20th century. I. Title.
NK2115.3.A76S56   1994
747.213—dc20   94-1453

Bulfinch Press is an imprint and trademark of Little, Brown and Company (Inc.)

Designed by Rick Horton
Typography by Tom and Shirley Hamilton
Printed and bound by Tien Wah Press

Frontispiece: Tom Joyce, Blacksmith

PRINTED IN SINGAPORE

Dedicated to the men and women who make things with their hands, minds, and hearts

CONTENTS

Authors' Note

If you are looking for the type of person who would best represent what we think of as the American character, the artist/craftsman is a wonderful candidate. Artist/craftsmen are men and women who are inventive, imaginative, adventurous, adaptable, self-reliant, and downright hardworking. They put forth a vision steeped in liveliness and usefulness, and seemingly through all adversity produce a well-conceived and crafted object. This is all accomplished with their hands, an achievement of which any mother could be proud. Through this process, much of their creative overflow finds its way into their homes, giving their environments a unique clarity of spirit and illuminating their personalities. In writing this book, we were given the opportunity to discover, explore, and enjoy their involvement in and dedication to their surroundings. We hope our explorations will help encourage all of us to examine the self-renewal, self-exploration, and self-contentment in a place called home.

—Tommy Simpson and Bill Seitz, 1994

Acknowledgments

We would like to express our fondest thank-yous to the wonderful people in this book who have generously given of their room and board, their time, and, most important, themselves.

We would also like to extend our thanks for their help and encouragement to Joanne Rapp at the Hand and Spirit Gallery in Scottsdale, Arizona; Martha Connell at the Martha Connell Gallery in Atlanta; Barbara Okun at the Okun Gallery in Santa Fe; Rick Snyderman at the Snyderman Gallery in Philadelphia; Scott Jacobson at the Leo Kaplan Modern Gallery in New York City; Mike and Carol Mendelson; and Kathy Vanoria and Mark Savoia at Connecticut Photographics in Danbury.

In addition, many thanks must go to Lisa Hammel for her help in writing this book; to Regina Ryan for her ability to make it all happen; to Janet Bush for her guidance, understanding, and direction; and to Amy Wilensky for her editing skills.

And finally, much love and thanks to Joanna and Amanda Seitz for their love and support and to Missy Stevens for her patience and support.

FOREWORD

Decorators' houses are usually beautifully decorated. Industrial designers' interiors are almost always crisply designed. Architects' places are often impressive integrations of furniture and accessories within a dominant architectural scheme. Artists' homes can be fascinating, but they are also sometimes merely eccentric, inward, or just plain ordinary.

But, a craftsman's house frequently looks like a wonderfully or oddly or surprisingly made object, as if it were one giant piece of furniture, or one vast tea set, or one grand tapestry, with a great intricacy of related parts that make up the whole.

Craftsmen have a great advantage in their possessing both a perceptive eye and the skill to carry out their visions. Imagine someone weaving roomfuls of rugs, making the dinnerware, the furniture, the silver centerpieces, the iron hardware—and doing all these things beautifully.

In an age that is moving beyond even the machine, we can all take pleasure in the fact that there are still people around with the skill to make wonderful objects by hand. And those of us who think we can only dream about the kinds of interiors these skilled craftsmen turn out for themselves may find it liberating to view what they have done. Much less bound by ideas of the way things are supposed to be, craftsmen make their intensely individual homes an object of creativity.

Most of us assemble our homes a little like a potluck dinner: we already have this on hand, someone gave us that, we needed one of these, that thing over there was a bargain, and this item right here was irresistible. Furnishing is an exercise combining inclination, impulse, and necessity, modified by the available funds. What is generally missing is an overview, an organizing principle beyond the dictates of taste or comfort. For craftsmen that principle is self-expression.

Craftsmen have a knack for turning their homes into extensions of themselves. What they acquire in their furnishings and how they arrange these things speaks of their values, their interests, and their sense of themselves in the world. This is undoubtedly what gives these interiors their distinctive personality, their feeling of being a direct reflection of the people who live in them. How do craftsmen do this? One of the ways is by filling their homes with objects that give evidence of the human mind and hand at work.

When craftsmen look for things for their home, they are guided by their respect for materials and good workmanship. This also shows up in their tendency to preserve what already exists. A delightful and well-made object is always looked upon with a kinder eye. And a possession that has a past, ancestral or otherwise, seems to be especially valued.

Craftsmen are not likely to spend much time shopping in the usual home-furnishings stores. Instead they haunt flea markets, junk shops, church benefits, yard sales, secondhand dealers, dusty antique shops, country auctions, and even country dumps or the discard piles on city streets.

Craftsmen also do a great deal of collecting. It is a way of bringing the larger world into their homes with objects from other times and other places, objects that give a sense of the myriad cultures of the world and the wonderful things people have thought up and made.

With all this amassing of the stuff of domestic life, how do craftsmen keep their homes from looking like the Museum of Improbable Finds? How do they avoid crowding and clutter? Craftsmen know how to achieve visual organization.

Once craftsmen have chosen their space and start gathering what they need and want, they seem to have a remarkable knack for arranging. Did any one of them ever stand in the middle of a room, temper rising, and wonder where to put the yet-another-thing they recently acquired for a sou? Apparently not.

For instance, Tommy Simpson and his wife, Missy Stevens, have ingeniously designed their house to include visual surprises everywhere, from how they line up their collections to how the chairs around the dining table form a ''matched set'' in which each chair is unique. Missy has some thoughts on dealing successfully with the complexity of one's surroundings: when faced with things in profusion or intensity—and this could be anything from a collection of objects to a grouping of furniture to flower beds—she establishes logical areas of containment.

Most craftsmen seem to put things where there is a reason to put them, not just on any random tabletop because the space happens to be there. And they arrange things compositionally: There is an aesthetic, a structural, and a material reason for what they do. Further, they always seem to be taking into consideration the context of a room, or even of an entire house; groupings are not just isolated arrangements, but always have something to do with the whole.

Lenore Tawney pulled together a large loft space by painting everything white, including the floor. But within that great white enclosure she created diverse "islands" for contemplation, work, storage, ordinary activity, beauty, mystery, and curiosity—all of which can be changed at will. It is an interior in slow flux that will never grow stale.

Diane Kempler and her husband, Bernhard, have a house in which every room is decorated in a different style or mood. In the center is a dramatic room opening up from an entry hall that announces who they are. This arrangement allows them to express the diversity in their lives and interests, but because they have made sure that each room or space has its own distinctive character, the result is a fascinating variety rather than an eclectic muddle.

The other golden rule craftsmen seem to practice in their homes is that when they go off in one unusual or strong direction, they balance that pull with elements that are more predictable, or quieter.

Bennett Bean has not been afraid to bring changes to his traditional New Jersey farmhouse. He has kept its character by using period furniture, retaining the original architecture and layout, and allowing generous space around everything such as would have prevailed in a late-eighteenth-century home. But he has also introduced many original touches—from squares of copper foil inlaid in the floor to artful linear arrange-

ments of things he likes to collect.

Jon Riis and Richard Mafong have made complex arrangements of artifacts from a number of exotic cultures, but they have maintained certain basics throughout—furniture with strong lines, consistent color schemes within each room or area, a limitation on textures, and quiet spaces as counterpoise.

Sam and Alfreda Maloof, whose house is a labyrinth of rooms and multiple levels, have unified its look with similar wall and floor treatments and furniture that is all from one master hand.

In sum, there have to be some strong consistencies to counterbalance diversity, and areas of containment within a liberality of space. These two rules of arrangement seem to make it possible to do almost anything and have it work.

I had the feeling that Tommy Simpson was strongly attracted to one of the most unlikely homes in this book, Lenore Tawney's loft. Although his house is arranged in a more conventional mode than Lenore's total study in living and making art, he sees a particular consonance between his own values and Lenore's as she has expressed them. Looked at in a broader way, what each has done is create an environment in which life, craft, aesthetic tastes, ideals, and personality all come together in a home. And in some way, this is true of every home Tommy and photographer Bill Seitz visited for this book.

I am about to introduce you to the home of Tommy Simpson and Missy Stevens. Then Tommy will take you on a tour of his own and of other craftsmen's homes around the country. Some of the craftsmen are very well known, some work more regionally. Each of their places seems integrated, connected—both complete and still growing. Each place is the product of an imagination that has been freed. In Tommy's words, "These craftsmen allow their joy to happen in their work and it goes everywhere around them—and into their houses."

—Lisa Hammel

Tommy Simpson
Woodworker
Missy Stevens
Weaver

Arriving in spring or summer one is distracted by the profusion of flowers billowing up to the front porch and sees only hints of their rural Connecticut house. Steeply pitched rooflines, weathered cedar clapboard siding, and an L-shaped front porch with an old-fashioned swing are glimpsed through the gnarled branches of an old crab apple tree. But once the door to the house is opened it becomes clear that this is not simply a recently constructed New England farmhouse.

Golden light and golden wood in an expanse of space greet the eye. The Simpson-Stevens home turns out to be an artfully conceived house that has managed to be two almost contradictory things at once — spacious and intimate. And the entire interior, from the front porch to the back deck, has been beautifully crafted.

Tommy, who has combined his original interest in painting and drawing with an attraction to woodworking, obtained his master's degree in fine arts from the Cranbrook Academy of Art in Bloomfield Hills, Michigan. He has taught for limited periods, and in recent years he has taken on some commissions, but he prefers opportunities that allow him time for his own work.

He is a perceptive man with a sharp eye, trained in the observation of the beautiful and the unusual. His own work has been called "fantasy furniture," an apt term in that he is always departing from design orthodoxy. He tries his hand at zany forms, at exuberant, abstract painted decoration. Or he combines archetypal forms with visual commentary to express a gently satirical point of view. The furniture and detailing he has fashioned for his own home share these qualities but are tamed for personal domestic consumption.

Among Missy's visible contributions to the house are her rugs, wall hangings, and upholstery covers, as well as her almost mystical "thread paintings." Missy, who received her degree in textile design from Boston University, has a subtle way with color. Her woven rugs attract a diverse range of tastes. A few years ago she added to her fiber-art repertoire when she discovered a Russian style of embroidery called *igolochkoy*. Using a hollow needle and a process rather like rug hooking, she combines two aesthetic interests — the desire to make pictures and a preference for working in fiber rather than paint.

Both Tommy and Missy value the preservation of the past and the work of human hands. Ancestral possessions can be found throughout the house. Much of the delightful effect of their home is owed to its fine workmanship and their many collections. Like many craftsmen, Tommy and Missy enjoy collecting the work of others, both friends and those unknown to them. As to detailing, a walk through their house brings visual adventures at every turn.

A sense of wonder at what the human hand is capable of fashioning is part of the pervasive personality of the house, along with its glowing maple floors, Missy's rugs, the high ceilings, the light streaming in through windows and skylights, careful placement of furniture and objects, and, of course, Tommy's ubiquitous furniture and detailing.

This house is notable not just for its visual delights and viability, its ingenuity and warmth, its originality and consistency, but also for its overall integration, and how thoroughly the house and garden reflect and realize the personalities of the owners.

Tommy, who has a fine eye for detail, also has insight into the whole. Furthermore, he has a feel for people and how they translate themselves and their work into a home. It is this perceptiveness that makes him an especially appropriate person to write this book.

— L. H.

Portrait | Tommy and Missy by the garage in their '39 Ford pickup truck.

Your home is inevitably an extension of yourself. What you choose to surround yourself with, the ways in which you modify and adapt your surroundings — whatever they may be — make a statement about how you live and who you are. For craftsmen, creating a home is a special challenge. It is already second nature for us to make things that express our opinions and observations, our likes and dislikes — and our homes can be our most personal creations. Missy and I have tried to create a home that reflects who we are, as craftsmen and as people. It has been an educational journey.

For a couple of years we had been looking to buy a house, but we couldn't find just the right one. We needed a house with enough space for both our studios — it is easy to see why so many artists live in lofts and converted barns — but many of the houses we saw were too huge and would cost a fortune to maintain. When a friend sold us some land in Connecticut, it seemed like the perfect opportunity to build a house ourselves. People tell horror stories about building their own homes, but we didn't find the process to be nearly as difficult as we had been led to believe. We began by drawing up wish lists, cutting pictures out of magazines, and visiting historic houses, measuring the proportions with our feet. Missy, who is very organized and determined, became the general contractor, and we drew up blueprints and hired a crew to do the framing. The head carpenter became a good friend. We still get together for dinner.

We quickly learned that the actual construction is not the most difficult part of building a house. You can always call an expert with your questions. The hard part is trying to get in all of your ideas without spending all of your money — we could have built three or four houses with all our ideas! Working within our budget, we had to pick and choose which elements best met our needs, the most important being enough studio space for us to work on large-scale projects. We wanted the house to be open yet cozy and, most important, to express our view of what we need to live and work. We also wanted it to be comfortable and welcoming and to fit in well with its rural New England surroundings.

The interior of the house was finished in phases, as time and our budget allowed, and sometimes it seemed as though we would never finish. For a while the house looked like a construction zone — full of machinery, untaped Sheetrock, plywood, and tools everywhere.

Eventually, though, all the clutter sorted itself out and we were able to see the results of all our work and planning and devote ourselves to the furnishing and arranging that helps give a house its character.

The house has a real New England feel. I sandblasted the glass panels on the top half of the Dutch front door with images of flowers and a moon and stars. On the bottom half I inlaid images of a cow, an apple, and another crescent moon in the wood. The wooden doorknob is of walnut and heart shaped. Throughout the house and yard, these images appear in unexpected places, from garage doors to bedposts. They are time-honored motifs, and we are glad they are part of a visitor's first impression of our home.

Inside, the house is not arranged conventionally into separate rooms. The central rectangle of the main floor is open, with certain areas — living area, dining area, casual eating area, kitchen — defined by groupings of furniture. There are also several very small rooms and little snug spots tucked behind, between, and at the ends of the large areas. We wanted a balance between little nooks and enclosures and wide-open spaces, to give a certain liveability to the design and a charm to the interior of the house.

In the living room area, my sunflower side table and matched chairs, with cowhide seat covers, are an inviting place to relax. The sofa I made sits on one of Missy's beautiful rugs before a large stone fireplace. If you look carefully, you will notice that here and there in the maple floor are little faces and figures staring back. I was offered a load of maple flooring at a good price, but it had knotholes in it. Still, it was too good an opportunity to pass up, so I covered the knotholes with wooden inlays of everything from birds to people. It was a lot of work, but we were pleased by the way it turned out.

To the right of the living room is the formal dining area. Its focal point is a table and chairs made of natural planks of English oak. I carved a fruit or vegetable name taken from a seed packet, such as "Dusky Wonder" (eggplant) and "Sweet Slice" (cucumber), into the back crest of each, so friends and family members could keep track of their favorite chair. The table sits before an old blue painted country cupboard originally from the Hudson River valley. Straight ahead is the open kitchen with its high skylight. And beyond the kitchen is the peaked roof of the casual eating area.

Living Room

Missy made the rug, the pillows (from Amish textile), and the woven picture hanging next to the stairs, entitled On the Road. I made the house-shaped fire screen and the andirons with help from Woodbury Blacksmiths, and the redware pot on the hearthstone with help from David Rubenstein. On top of the mantel is a row of many tiny glass containers holding sand from all over the world that we have collected or friends have given us. The pegs set into the mantel are meant to hold mittens and socks that are wet from the snow and need to dry.

Detail

One of Missy's thread paintings and three dolls — two antiques and one that I made.

This area began its life as a screened porch, but we discovered that even in the summer there was only a limited period when you could sit outside in New England—it's too rainy or hot or cold or overcast. So we decided to create a room indoors that felt like the outdoors year-round, but without the sleet and humidity and mosquitoes. We wanted this area to provide warmth and light to the whole first floor of the house, and we knew we would spend a good deal of time there enjoying the view, so we made sure to put in plenty of windows on both sides of the room. And with the windows open, air can flow through as on a screened porch. Our collection of forty teapots is lined up around the top of the windows, and my round table is in the center of the room.

The fairly small kitchen, between the informal and formal dining areas, was one of the more difficult parts of the house to get right. In a kitchen you have to work around the appliances. You can't just move things around any which way—there are definite limitations. We got some child-sized blackboards from the Boston Children's Museum, and I used them to make doors for the cabinets above the sink—they are a good place to leave messages and record thoughts. I made the rest of the cabinets from scraps of hickory and chestnut left over from other jobs, and framed them in cherry. Opposite the kitchen is a little pantry where we answer the phone, keep the cookbooks, hang the outdoor togs, and cover the walls and shelves with all sorts of things.

The door to my current studio is on one side of the dining area; the door on the other side leads to our bedroom. We made one of our biggest mistakes when building the bedroom. It was just part of the learning process, I guess. We made the ceiling so uncomfortably high—more appropriate for a choir singing a hallelujah chorus than for two people trying to get a night's sleep —that we had to lower it. It all worked out, though, and we turned the leftover space into a storage area.

Although most of the house is concentrated on the main floor, there is a guest room downstairs, at ground level, where the land slopes toward a pond. At the other end a wing adjoins the house at right angles, suggesting a courtyard as you approach the house. This wing used to be my woodworking shop until it became too small and we had to construct another shop in the back. The old shop is now my painting studio and a place to display our work.

The pieces I make in my woodworking shop are meant to express joy and spontaneity. I take formal

Dining Room   l e f t

Everything in this room has been crafted by hand. I built the English oak table and the cherry-wood chairs, and Missy made the chair cushions. David Rubenstein and I made and painted all of the pottery. Missy wove the carpet from corduroy rags and also made, from fabric and beads, the row of heads sitting on the ledge of the blue step-back cupboard. I sand-blasted the glass vase in the center of the table, and Missy wove the thread paintings on the wall. I built the doors, which have the word "HOME" spelled out across the top, one letter on each corner (only the "O" and the "M" are visible). I also made the figured door handles in the shapes of Missy and myself.

Detail   r i g h t

Sitting on the cabinet ledge are a row of fabric heads and figures Missy made. The skeleton hanging from the knob is papier-mâché from Mexico. We made the garden sign below it that reads "peas & Quiet" for the shop at the Museum of American Folk Art.

Detail   a b o v e

This curio cabinet in the dining area is my commentary on the inveterate collector (and a little spoof on Missy and myself as well). Items it holds include a miniature fence, a wooden coat hanger decorated with a carved heart, antique wooden chains, a pogo stick in the shape of a cross, a silver-leafed crescent moon, a chair in a glass bottle, a stuffed leather head, and an inscribed fungus.

elements of design that are steeped in tradition and apply my own vocabulary to them. Sometimes people call my work "fantasy furniture," and I think they mean that I don't always adhere to a generally agreed-upon or traditional style or method. However, the furniture and detailing I have made in my woodshop for my own home is more utilitarian in many cases than the artwork I exhibit and sell.

Missy creates unusual and beautiful weavings—rugs, wall hangings, upholstery covers—as well as "thread paintings," pictures made of cloth and silk thread. Her studio is a loft that for a long time lacked a normal access. Eventually I was able to build the open staircase that now leads to it. Each of the balusters is a different stylized stem-and-flower shape, and there are stars cut into the walnut newel. There are three sections of treads, made of three different woods: oak, cherry, and spalted maple. I discovered that I had just enough oak for one set of treads, so I changed the wood for the next two sections. The main post supporting the stairs is the trunk of an oak tree. This is particularly appropriate because for a long time you had to climb a ladder to get to the studio, and Missy felt as if she were working in a tree house.

Floor-to-ceiling shelves hold large spools of the thread Missy uses for the warps of her woven rugs, as well as miscellaneous thread she has collected over the years. One whole wall is covered with the mostly recycled corduroy strips, in a multitude of colors, with which she weaves her rugs. Another wall is hung with framed arrangements of everything from button samples to antique lace and Victorian calling cards. Her work-table is covered with hundreds of spools of cotton, silk, and rayon thread that she uses in her thread paintings.

An old family portrait on the studio wall includes Missy's paternal great-grandmother, a great needle-woman. Missy feels she has inherited her forebears' interests and abilities. Her other grandmother loved to garden, and Missy is the head gardener in our house-hold. We maintain three different gardens: an old-fashioned English cottage garden near the house, where flowers spill onto the paths; a garden of vegeta-bles, melons, and berries on a terraced level below the house; and the peach and plum trees and flowering shrubs that border the lawn. We love to bring flowers from the gardens into the house.

Much of the furniture and detailing in our house is of our own hands, but we also collect the work of other craftsmen, such as Wendell Castle's impressive floriform cutting-board table in the kitchen and Laura Wilensky's hand-painted ceramic tea set. Our shared love for nostalgia and a respect for the traditions of the past have led us to collect antiques as well, like the stepped country cabinet in the dining room, the pie safe in the main bedroom, and the jelly cupboard in the guest room. Inherited pieces, yet another connection to the past, figure prominently in and around the house. In the living room, my great-grandparents' footstools and the fireplace lintel (made from a butternut tree on my great-grandfather's farm) bring up fond memories for me; Missy's grandmother's birdbath sits in the center of the lower garden. And finally, we are both inveterate collectors and have shared and individual collections throughout the house, from spongeware mixing bowls to alphabet plates, teddy bears, feathers, shells, antique quilts, samplers, mittens, buttons, cloth doll heads, and the forty teapots above the kitchen windows. The amazing variety of solutions people find in making things has always fascinated us, and we would like nothing more than to have our home to be seen as a tribute to the work of human hands.

It is a most rewarding feeling to look around your home at what you have accomplished and realize you are still in one piece. It has been hard work creating a home, but it was and is an unforgettable experience. I have my own opinions on what gives our house personality—the detailing, the rich natural materials, the sense of history, and the devotion to things made by hand—and Missy has hers. The feeling that our house "fits" us and our lives is proof to us that we have succeeded in creating not just a house, but a home.

We are about to take a tour of the homes of craftsmen who have succeeded in creating homes that express their work and their personalities. Each home is unique and highly personal and represents for these craftsmen—as we hope our home does for us—their creativity, their creations, and themselves.

Kitchen

The kitchen is partly tucked out of sight so that dirty dishes are invisible to dinner guests. The counter in the foreground begins next to the stove (unseen, opposite the sink) and curves around the wall into the enclosed porch and eating area. Under the blackboard cabinets is the plate rack I made to hold our dinnerware, which was all made by Bill Sax. I grain-painted the refrigerator to look like wood. The plates arranged on the wall are English children's alphabet plates, one of our many collections. The beams above the kitchen were rescued from a barn torn down in Bethlehem, Connecticut. Another example of salvage is the handle of the refrigerator, a piece of grapevine Missy found at an arboretum in Boston just as it was about to be discarded. I made the brown standing plate, Emma's water dish, and the pastel in the center of the wall. Above the platter, little wooden folk art figures surround a knitted black doll from Maine.

Enclosed Porch and Eating Area

The door on the right wall leads to a deck. The windows at the back face the woods. I made the stools with zebrawood seats that pull up to the counter. Missy wove the rug and made the cushions and pillows for the window seat. The vase in the center of the table is by contemporary glass-blower George Thiewes. I made the crescent moon hanging from the rafters and the structural, flower-shaped post that bisects the triangular window at the gable. The floors here, as elsewhere in the house, are figured maple. The tall gray object on the right, near the door to the deck, is the first grandfather clock I ever made.

Kitchen, Detail

This cabinet holds our mixing bowl collection, part of which originally belonged to my mother. The mottled surface of the cabinet is similar to the general pattern on the spongeware. The sunflower, seen on the upper part of the cabinet between the glass doors, is another design we especially like. The cabinet stands opposite the kitchen; the eating area is off to the right. Daisy poses on a bench I made for her, which is covered with one of Missy's fabrics. Above the bench are two of my paintings from the early seventies. To the left, just beyond Missy's rugs, is the entry to the pantry. In the doorway, on the floor, is my tall black ceramic dog pitcher.

Bedroom left

The built-in, all-purpose storage unit under the clerestory windows was put in just a few years ago, part of a small addition to the house. Glimpsed to the left of the cabinets is an open door that leads to a little office and a tiny library. On the left, an unusual storage cabinet stands next to French doors that lead to the deck and an outdoor shower. The indoor master bathroom is opposite the cabinet, behind the bookshelves seen at the extreme left. My mother, Poggy, made the needlepoint cover on the chair, and I made the wooden ark sitting on the lintel.

Bedroom right

I built the pencil-post bed from antique English oak and mahogany, and Missy made the linen canopy. The quilt is one from our collection. The blanket at the foot of the bed is an American antique wool coverlet. The hooked rug beside the bed, which reads "Dream," is from my home state of Illinois. Every inch of the wall-to-wall carpeting in this large room was handwoven by Missy; she also made the upholstery for my foot-of-the-bed bench. I grain-painted the night tables, one of which holds a pair of sleigh mittens. Above the table with the mittens is a framed *retablo* from New Mexico. The barn ladder on the wall next to the clock leads up to a storage area off Missy's loft studio. We made the large round porcelain plates above the bed together at the Kohler Art and Industry Program in Wisconsin. The door next to the ladder leads to the dining room.

20

Bedroom, Detail

I made this splay-legged curio cabinet, with the toothy apron trim, out of maple, English oak, and cherry. It holds family mementos, photos, and other memorabilia, including a love letter from my great-grandmother to my great-grandfather and a box that belonged to a Shaker ancestor. It also holds Missy's childhood teddy bear, a ceramic bear she made in grade school, and a profusion of bears we have collected.

Guest Bedroom

On the lower level of the house, a few steps from the side lawn that leads to a neighbor's placid pond, is the guest bedroom. A tin-and-wood scarecrow guards the bed, which is covered with an antique quilt and coverlet. I made the "poem" jars with David Rubenstein. Missy made the polka-dot pillows from old grain sacks. The walls are wooden panels that have been sponge-painted. The antique bed is iron.

23

Dave Williamson
Jewelry Maker/Ceramist

Roberta Williamson
Jewelry Maker

Just as their house is welcoming, so are the Williamsons. It is not hard to feel comfortable in their company. To them their house is much more than a place to come home to for dinner. It is central to their lives, and house symbols show up both in their work and in their decor. For these two, everything is interrelated: their relationship, their mutual memories, where they work, and what they work at.

The Williamsons' home, in Ohio, is comfortable and feels lived in; it does not look as though it has undergone major renovation. When they first moved into the three-bedroom home, they stripped it down to the Sheetrock walls, removed the carpeting and plywood paneling, and took it back to what Dave calls "plain and simple." The Williamsons moved into the house in 1976 with the idea that it would be an interim arrangement, perhaps for three years, while Dave got settled in his college teaching job. They have been there ever since.

The house is a one-story ranch set well back from the street. It has all the features they need: a sufficient number of bedrooms—the master bedroom, daughter Lauren's room, and a guest room—and enough space for dining, relaxing, and entertaining. As jewelers, they do not need a large place to work; the former two-car garage does quite well as a workshop. Behind the house is a large, private yard that abuts a municipal park. The garden is pleasantly landscaped and offers the serenity of a tree-girded fishpond.

The Williamsons' home is so central a symbol in their lives that it is even featured in the decor. When they put together the family room a few years ago, they built the fireplace surround in the shape of the house and faced it with local river stones. The house also appears frequently as an image in their work.

Roberta's attraction to jewelry making began in childhood. Her father and grandfather were sheet-metal workers, and she grew up playing with metal scraps. Also, she was a petite child and became accustomed to surroundings and possessions on a small scale— the delicacy of jewelry making seemed natural to her. She became accustomed early on to handling tools, and while still a youngster she began making small metal items that she dressed up with gold paint.

She met Dave at Northern Illinois University, where she was studying art. Dave signed up for a few art courses himself. He tried ceramics and metalsmithing, and he became very interested in working with clay. After attending graduate school together in Virginia, the couple settled in Ohio, where Dave was offered a job teaching ceramics at a local college.

Roberta extended her jewelry repertoire when their daughter, Lauren, was born. She began making charm necklaces as a practical approach to the problem of trying to work while taking care of an infant. She could work on one small unit at a time, and still jump up whenever she had to attend to the baby.

Living Room | The Empire couch and the chest behind it were bought locally and the couch was reupholstered. The little red-and-silver chair on the right was given to Roberta by her mother when she was a child. On the stools next to the chair are a collection of compasses and three silver frames Dave made. On the twig table, the ceramic lamp-base under the black shade was made by Dave and shows images of Dave and Roberta. On top of the chest are pieces by Dave (at left) and another ceramist flanking two African headdresses. The two stem glasses in front of Dave's vase are a prize the couple won at a Milwaukee craft fair. A Pennsylvania Dutch quilt hangs over the back of the sofa.

Living Room, Detail

The table in front of the windows overlooking the backyard neatly displays some of the Williamsons' smaller treasures. A number of them are Japanese, including a kimono-clad doll, a pen case, a signature stamp, bonsai pruning shears, graduated bowls, and ceramic bells. Also among the myriad objects are a number of wooden boxes by craftsman Paul Summer, pins by Dave and Roberta (including some designed by their daughter), and two sets of little boats, one group on a red lacquered Japanese tray, the other set in a row on the windowsill.

Living Room, Detail

Some of the boxes the Williamsons collect double as storage containers. The metal toolbox on the table at the front was made by Roberta's father as an apprentice's project, as was the metal star sitting at the edge of the box at the base of the pile. The tall wooden object to the left of the boxes is an African pestle. On the wall hangs a framed blowup of a small painting by Lauren.

Living Room, Detail

The modern coffee table in front of the Empire sofa holds a ceramic bowl by Dave filled with marble hearts carved by a stonecutter. (The Williamsons are particularly fond of the heart as a design motif.) Next to it, a carved wooden African boat holds some of their dice collection.

Living Room, Detail

The wood and glass case against the wall of the living room was a store display case the couple bought at an auction. It serves well to display some of their varied objects, among them an elaborately carved African headdress and a group of wooden dolls said to be from the Micronesian islands in the Pacific. These are grouped beneath two reverse paintings on glass that the Williamsons liked but were unable to discover anything about. Items inside the case—which is flanked by more of Dave's ceramics—include African and Native American baskets and gourds.

A few years ago, when Roberta became ill and could not fulfill her production commitment for shops and upcoming crafts fairs, Dave went back to jewelry making to help out. When Roberta recovered her health, they found they liked working together so well that they decided to continue. Dave still teaches, but he does not work as much in clay anymore. The couple find that their exchange of information, as a working process, keeps fresh ideas coming. Also, there are two heads instead of one, which brings an expanded perspective to what they make.

Many shared experiences, memories, and symbols of their feelings for each other and others they love find their way into the Williamsons' work. Their beloved dog Petie died, and now dogs keep showing up in their jewelry. The fondly remembered canine will soon be memorialized in an image on a metal fountain they have designed and plan to have made for the lawn. Other symbols that show up in stylized form, signifying friendship, affection, love, and both sad and happy memories, include the house—of course—and hearts, hands, leaves, and old buttons. These symbols are not always easily interpreted by others, but Dave and Roberta know what language they speak. They have recently added what Roberta calls a narrative element to some of their work, in which a design may include a private message engraved on a silver memo page. Their work is also influenced by the images presented in the objects they collect.

Roberta and Dave have arranged the things they collect in such an appealing and personal way that it is clear they are dealing with things they love. The house is full of individual touches that offer feasts for the eye. Even the bathrooms are fair game as settings. Among the many objects they enjoy collecting are Japanese artifacts, from dolls to bonsai pruning scissors. These are set out on a table in the living room amid many other small things. They collect such variety simply because they find so many things attractive and appealing. Anything that speaks of the sea is another example, such as little wooden boats, beach stones, fish designs. They also collect dice, which they use in their jewelry—they like the design, and dice are just the right size for their pieces. And perhaps these symbols of risk, adventure, exoticism, and the unknown add a little spice to the gentleness of their daily lives.

Nothing this couple owns gets squirreled away. Whatever they own is "out there," as Dave says, ready to be contemplated and used.

Guest Bedroom, Detail

This is a close-up of a pin on the dressing table, a valentine that Roberta made for Dave. The words around the silver rim read "Stuff I love about you." On the back of the pin are some of the particulars: "your eyes, your lips," and so forth.

Master Bedroom

The master bedroom centers around a modern pencil-post bed. The quilt at its foot is by contemporary quilter Nancy Crow. On the near side of the bed is a bamboo table covered with wooden whimsies carved by prisoners and some Michigan fish lures. Above the pillows, three old plates in a blue-and-white willow pattern hang on the wall above flowers in twig baskets. The tall chest on the left is an old German music cabinet with a tin battleship on top of it, and on the wall above it is half a wooden boat hull, a gift from a friend. The open door leads to the master bathroom, which is decorated with a number of little boats, among other things.

Family Room, Detail

The fireplace surround in the family room was made by Roberta and Dave with the help of a mason. In warm weather the hearth is host to a toy wooden barn that repeats the basic house shape. The little pile of stones on the right near the sunflowers were gathered and arranged as a souvenir of a well-remembered visit to Nantucket. The ceramic piece on the floor is Dave's. At the center of the mantel is a plate, decorated with a salmon, by Mara Superior. The Williamsons met and became friends with the Superiors at craft fairs, and they also know Thomas Mann. One of Mara's porcelain dogs stands to the right of the plate; figures by Jack Earl, a well-known Ohio ceramist, are on the left. The little niche in the center of the fireplace surround holds three sterling silver figures made by Dave and Roberta. And speaking of dogs, Buzz, the family's toy poodle, poses in an oversize, floral-covered armchair the Williamsons had made locally.

Family Room, Detail

On the other side of the armchair is a twig table (the couple are particularly fond of twig and branch tables) that holds some of their jewelry designs, including a dog surveying a pile of dice and a little boat filled with stones. French doors lead out to the backyard.

Portrait | The Williamsons with a large sculpture on the grounds of their home.

Backyard | A small fish pond adds a refreshing note to a garden where the
outdoor furniture has been chosen with care. An Adirondack bench,
looking like an incipient spider web, sits near an apple tree and
a border of flowers. The birdhouse in the background—
often a home to squirrels—was made locally.

Bennett Bean

Bennett Bean is a ceramist well known for his brilliantly colored pots, with gilt interiors, that seem to have been put together in sections and chunks. He and his wife, Cathy Bao Bean, live in an eighteenth-century farmhouse in a rural corner of New Jersey. Cathy was a philosophy teacher; she now manages their business affairs. She is presently writing a book on her childhood in this country after her father, a diplomat, was caught here following the Communist takeover in China.

Their house—and Bennett's experiences in remodeling it—represents one of the main themes of this book: A craftsman moves into an ordinary place. Then he uses his skill, knowledge, and responsive eye to transform the house into a one-of-a-kind creation. And all this is done with a great team anyone can hire —ingenuity and sweat.

Bennett spent his earliest years, during World War II, on the army bases where his father was a doctor. Sometimes he and his mother would visit a great-aunt who lived in Cincinnati, surrounded by what Bennett remembers as "beautiful objects." The contrast between the sameness of the army quarters and the uniqueness of his great-aunt's house left a deep impression on him and led to his later conviction that objects should be made to be beautiful as well as useful and "artistic." Also, because of the war, he grew up in a "world of women." He was introduced at an early age to the subtleties of the arts and to more than the usual little boy's universe of guns, cowboys, and baseball.

He believes he chose clay as his medium because it is "both a mind and body material." Making pots engages him physically, but it calls on his intellect and his aesthetic instincts as well. He also likes to have something at day's end, something he can actually hold on to.

Although Bennett is best known in the craft world for his pots, he has another line of work that draws on his pragmatic side. He makes modular, add-on terra-cotta columns, each about eighteen inches high. The capitals that top the columns are cast. He worked with a manufacturer to design an extruding device so he could make the columns himself, which he now does in the downstairs workshop of his barn. Upstairs are his gallery and his showroom.

It was actually this large barn that sold him on the ten-acre property. He recalls turning to Cathy when he saw it and saying with a smile on his face: "This is it. Now how do we pay for it?" He might just as well have said "How do we fix it up?" because the house was a handyman's delight: the front door was dangling from its hinges and the walls in the attic looked like venetian blinds—you could see right out through the laths.

They bought the house in 1970. The reconstruction was done on a neediest-case-first basis over a period of twenty years. One day the granite-and-slate hearthstone in the dining room fell into the basement. Clearly, it was time for a new floor. Bennett replaced the old floor with rosewood, into which he set some copper-foil blocks in a subtle design that glows with the light reflecting in the gleam of the wood and the soft sheen of the metal.

The badly cracked walls also needed attention. Ordinarily he might have knocked them down and put up Sheetrock, or settled for replastering and painting, or covered them with a wall fabric to hide the defects. But Bennett decided to go with the flow: he would give them interest, elegance, and age, and make them look like old weathered walls in an Italian villa. Potters love encrustation. It was labor-intensive work, but

Dining Room | An oval dining table is centered on a deeply gleaming rosewood floor inlaid with copper foil–covered blocks. Georgian candlesticks are in the center of the table; rush-seated Hitchcock chairs are around it. Next to the spider-legged tea table against the wall on the right is a standing Arts and Crafts period lamp. On the opposite wall is an Italian painting by an anonymous artist; Bennett made the gold leaf–covered frame. Under it, two of Bennett's bowls sit on the Sheraton-style table. On the mantel, a George Ohr pot sits near a samurai sword. The paired portraits above the mantel are eighteenth-century American.

the finished walls looked old and beautiful. He is now trying the textured approach on the surface of hanging cabinets. He made a simple wood case and painted it with clay slip (liquid clay), using a sponge instead of a brush. It hangs in the living room over the mantel, holding family photographs.

In reconstructing his house, Bennett was influenced by the simplicity of its old-fashioned design. It gave him a viewpoint for the entire project—a way to approach making it his own (Cathy leaves the house to Bennett). I think if you went through this house slowly, you would get a clear picture of Bennett, a man who treasures both tradition and imagination.

You gain a sense from the house that Bennett is one of a long line of Beans. Some of the furnishings in his home have been passed down to him through his family, and they maintain and illuminate his family history. He has a grandfather clock in the hall that was actually owned by his grandfather. It even has a handwritten message from the past inside it—the instructions on how to wind it.

Bennett's house is a result of many influences: American cultural history, his own heritage, his and other craftsmen's skills, and his numerous interests. American antiques, both bought and inherited, are supplemented by furnishings found in flea markets or purchased from pickers—the "finders" of the antique business. His own work is everywhere, but there is also the work of other craftsmen, like the turned-wood bowl by David Ellsworth, and the chair in the living room he made with Daniel Mack, a craftsman known for his twig-and-branch furniture. Exchange is frequent in the world of craftsmen. Bennett also has some work by George Ohr, a remarkable, late-nineteenth-century potter who was ahead of his time.

Like the Ohr pieces, all of Bennett's collections are unusual and unique. They range from early-twentieth-century American art pottery to Native American pelt scrapers. Unlike the houses of some people who collect (or just plain accumulate), Bennett's home is uncluttered, spacious, and airy. Everything has its place.

The house also holds visual surprises. Bennett likes unusual materials and the effects of combining them. He rejuvenates antique paintings he unearths at flea markets by brightly gilding the frames or shelves he makes for them. He sets his pots on pedestals that relate to the piece displayed, and he groups objects on a tabletop or on the floor as if they just happened to come together. He makes other objects interrelate in a purposeful way, such as the small maritime collection that sits with other treasures in the upper hallway.

Living Room

The living room, seen here from the center hall, has a wall painted with so many layers that its appearance depends partly on the light. Above the mantel is a hanging cabinet Bennett made. Its interior is sponge-painted in a faux tortoise-shell effect, and its frame is gilded. It contains family memorabilia, including photos of Bennett's grandfather and an uncle. The round end table to the left of the mantel was made by a great-uncle. The tall twig-backed chair is the result of a collaboration between Bennett and contemporary furniture maker Daniel Mack. The sofa is covered with a Peruvian poncho. On a chest in front of the sofa is a shallow wooden rice tub holding gilded forms. The ash floor of the living room blends well with the maple floor of the hall, which has rosewood inlays (not seen). Next to the living room doorway is another one of Bennett's creations, on a pedestal he made from scrap granite and acrylic. The straight-back chair on the left side of the door is a country chair with a new seat made with Shaker-style webbing.

Detail a b o v e

In a corner of the living room, where the sunlight changes the look of the wall color to a soft peach tone, a cast-bronze piece by Bennett, entitled *Bird*, sits atop a pedestal. On one side of it is a southern country chair; on the other, a basket filled with duck decoys that Bennett bought in Nova Scotia.

Detail b e l o w

Atop an old-fashioned jelly cupboard in the living room is a clutch of gilded ceramic shapes Bennett made, sitting in a wooden Japanese rice tub. The two small figures to the right of the tub are made from horn and belonged to Bennett's family. Bennett airbrushed a design on the earthenware platter in back.

Aging the Walls

Through trial and error, Bennett worked out a way to paint walls so that they look as if they were part of an old Italian villa. The living room was the site of his first experiment. A slightly textured surface was the result of applying about fourteen coats, of varied colors, of a paint almost as thick as toothpaste. The dining room was next, and the process went much faster. Five applications of paint — in combinations of green, gray, and blue — were patted on with a sponge; each coat was left to dry before the next was applied. The walls were then finished with a transparent polyurethane tinted a reddish gray, followed by a second glazing coat of bluish gray polyurethane cut very thin. By the time he got to the hallway, Bennett had the procedure down to only three coats, including the polyurethane, to achieve the desired effect of old mellow walls. Here, Bennett's collection of ceramics by George Ohr rests on a gilded shelf.

Kitchen, Detail   a b o v e

A kitchen desk is covered with some of Bennett's miscellaneous collections, including two huge teeth (possibly belonging to a whale), a row of Indian pelt scrapers made from stones that have been sharpened and roughened on one end, an old whetstone, a little Yixing teapot next to a turtle shell, some small meteorites, and a working rotary telephone.

Kitchen Greenhouse   l e f t

The kitchen greenhouse is a delightful spot for meals — it offers a view over the landscaped grounds and gardens. Two of Bennett's terra-cotta columns form the base of the table; its round top is an aluminum sheath over a wood core. The metal chairs around the table are from an old hotel. Bennett arranges flowers in a pot made with an early Renaissance inlaid-slip technique and decorated with figures after nineteenth-century multiple-frame photographs by Eadweard Muybridge.

Kitchen   r i g h t

The kitchen has cherry floors and cabinets Bennett designed. The shelves above the sink and counter hold a mix of American and Canadian pottery and more of Bennett's work. Although the walnut table was made by someone else, Bennett designed it, finished it, and inlaid a snake into the surface. The chairs are modern in a light wood. The backsplash above the sink and counter is made with European majolica tiles he found.

Salvaging things that someone else would have thrown out and recognizing what can be saved or reused is characteristic of a number of craftsmen. Bennett, who is interested in how things are put together, once bought a wooden Buddha with the cast-iron head jammed down into its body. He took it to the local hospital to have it x-rayed, and everyone thought he was looking for hidden jewels. He just wanted to find out how to get the head out and back into its original position. It is now sitting on an old nailed chest in the downstairs hall.

Bennett uses scraps and chunks of granite from a nearby monument company for all kinds of projects. The smaller pieces have turned up as paving stones in a path and building stones in an embankment. Now he is using odd pieces to build a long wall along the road's boundary with his property.

Bennett is his own landscape designer. The outside and the inside of the house are all one to him — a variety of design problems. He has put ponds and gardens and walkways all over the grounds. The biggest difference between his crafts and his work on the house and grounds is time. You make a pot, fire it, and hold it up and decide whether or not you like it. But it can take months, even years of labor to see the mistakes you have made in a room or a garden. For Bennett, his projects all have "legs" — their own momentum, an inherent energy that keeps everything in his life in forward motion.

Albert Paley

Metalsmith

Even before you park you have decided that the house you are approaching would have to belong to a sculptor —it has that kind of visual presence. A deeply curved enclosing roof comes down over the house like a cape, while angled dormers butt through the top of it. The unusual brick-and-shingle house, a rose color in sunlight with a deep-gray roof, turns out to be even more of a surprise inside.

The front door is opened and you are welcomed into the library. The huge house in upstate New York that Albert and his wife, Frances, bought in 1981—and worked on for ten years—was originally the carriage house on a large estate. It was also the stable for the owner's racehorses. The library, so full of great art books that you could spend months in there reading, was the old tack room; it still has the original glass cases that held equestrian equipment. Now the cases hold books.

The library opens into a large hall. Off to the right is an area that includes a guest bedroom and a storage area. To your left you glimpse the expansive space that serves as living room, dining room, and open kitchen. The house covers seven thousand square feet.

Upstairs is the master bedroom, which looks out on the Rochester cityscape, and Frances and Albert's drawing studio. Frances works full-time as a psychotherapist, and does volunteer work in the community. Their sixty-foot-long studio, painted mostly white and with the same smooth maple floors found throughout the house, has ceilings that look like origami.

Albert and Frances have changed little of the original architecture of the first floor. They have chosen not to enclose the big spaces where horses once munched hay and carriages were sheltered from the weather. Both Albert and Frances feel most at home in large, open spaces.

Albert's initial craft was goldsmithing, and soon after school he began to establish a name for himself with his distinctive baroque style of jewelry. In 1974 Albert won a design competition to build the portals for the Smithsonian's Renwick Gallery in Washington, D.C., the nation's official craft museum. This commission was the turning point in his professional life. Not long afterward, he started working with forged iron— he is a self-taught blacksmith and sculptor. When he decided he wanted to work in iron instead of gold and silver, he read books and went to museums, picking up techniques along the way. He had estimated that the 1,200-pound, hand-forged Renwick gates would take him 400 hours to finish. Working with an assistant, the project took 3,500 hours.

Albert became known nationally for the large architectural elements he was building for both private and government sources. Later, with a major commission from an arts center in Houston, Texas, he began to fabricate outsize sculpture as well. He has both a forge and a successful fabricating plant in Rochester, where he still does all of the designing, but not as much of the hands-on work as he would like to.

Albert's workplaces are big by necessity—dramatic things happen at a forge, and people move around with great speed and excitement. Having this setting as part of his everyday life has had an undeniable influence on what kind of surroundings make Albert feel at home.

From the beginning Albert has made furniture. Not surprisingly, these pieces are more imposing than Chippendale side chairs, for example. In a tamer setting, even one of his plant stands would be liable to take over a whole room. And, like most craftsmen, Albert has his work all around the house. So there is a logic to the large dramatic building he and Frances found, restored, and made into their home.

House Exterior, Front | The house is a former carriage house and racing stable built in 1892 on the grounds of an estate. The bedrooms and drawing studio are in the dormers. The car parked outside is Albert's 1966 Austin Healy.

It is hard to believe, looking around at the original, gleaming, off-white ceramic tile walls, the mellowness of the polished floors and the custom-made wood trim, the warmth of the Oriental rugs, the flowers in vases everywhere, and the overall order in this large space, that the house was a wreck when they bought it. For much of the 1920s the house was a film studio and lab. It is not clear what happened after that, but the tons of debris that Albert and Frances had to clear away even included old automobiles. Although they had help from friends and from Albert's employees, it was a major commitment for them to restore the house, and it absorbed much of their spare time and energy for ten years. Their decision to try to restore it to its original form—because they so admired the unique architectural character of the building—involved many problems. They discovered, for example, that the brick had been custom-made when the house was built in 1892. But because they wanted to keep the house as close as possible to its original architecture, they replaced everything with at least a reasonable equivalent.

They did adjust part of the living room, "to give it a human scale"—not by lowering the fourteen-foot ceiling, but by raising part of the floor four feet. The 2,400-square-foot room full of iron accessories, solid furniture, and statuary is majestic. Albert and Frances like the solid masculine style of Gustav Stickley's oak furniture, which is in all the rooms. American Arts and Crafts designs, such as Stickley's, are of the same period as the house. They also collect animal skulls and antlers. Albert says he likes the curving forms of the bare bones, and his own ironwork often mimics the twisting, twisted antlers. They have a display case full of turn-of-the-century European art pottery in the big hall. And most of the busts and smaller sculptures they own are from the same period. There is a notable consistency to what the Paleys have collected—most everything is from the same era as the house.

Each year Albert brings home one or two of his pieces to keep as a record in a developing archive. If he did not do this, there would be only paper and photographic records of his past work. And having the work at home, Albert says, gives him time to reflect on it and see its strengths and weaknesses.

Albert has an Austin Healy, a classic British sports car, he has lovingly maintained since 1966. Someone who owns an Austin Healy, a car that many would see as the epitome of a classic era for British sports cars, is someone who is compelled by the character of the design. For Albert it also represents his sentimental side, and it has become a fixture in his life. Both he and Frances seem to fit with their house, which they see as something of a sanctuary and a shield against the long, gray winters. Its grandness, spaciousness, and striking appeal echo their expansive personalities.

This dwelling had never been a home before Albert and Frances bought it, at least not for the two-footed. Perhaps it was too daunting an undertaking for anyone else. Maybe you have to have Albert's vision and toughness to see that it will work.

Main Hallway

A German clock stands against the original stairway leading to the second floor. The living room can be glimpsed beyond. The light fixtures are Art Deco and came from an office building. The coat rack in the near hallway holds twenty-five coats. The door on the right leads to the downstairs bathroom, which used to be the room into which hay was deposited through a chute from above.

Table in Main Hallway

The American Arts and Crafts style table is covered with odds and ends the couple has collected, including building and tombstone fragments, a New Guinean mask, and a French oil painting of a nude. Animal skulls are both under and over the table. The chairs to the left are turn-of-the-century Austrian with embossed leather upholstery. Above the chairs is an airbrushed-watercolor-and-pen-and-ink drawing by Frances called *The Wave*.

Library/Hall far left

The front entryway leads
directly into the library,
which is filled with art books,
new and old. The woodwork is
original, as are the glassed-in
bookcases, where equestrian
equipment was kept. An early-
twentieth-century fey statuette
decorates the library table.
The door at back leads
to the main hallway.

Side Hallway near left

Glass display cases in the
side hallway hold the couple's
collection of turn-of-the-century
European pottery and metalwork.
A Stickley rocker sits next to one
of Albert's tables. The candlesticks are German. The door leads
out to the garage.

Sideboard   l e f t

An assemblage of insects under glass from the Malay Archipelago sits beside yet another skull on an iron desk or sideboard made by Albert. To the right of the insects is a Viennese iron clock. Above the clock is a print of a well-known painting by the late-nineteenth-century British artist Lawrence Alma-Tadema. On the left, perpendicular to the desk, is a red-enameled iron stove from Vermont. Albert made the fireplace tools beside it. The stove is faithfully guarded by a cast-iron dog from about 1840.

Living Room   b e l o w

Albert and Frances pose on one of a pair of Stickley oak settles that flank the three-sectioned window. The window was originally the door through which carriages entered. The impressive torchère is by Albert, as are the small side table and the coffee table.

Living Room Entrance   l e f t

One of the three Paley dogs, Alphonse, sleeps in the well area at the entrance to the huge living room, which measures forty by sixty feet. He is named for Alphonse Mucha, the Czech Art Nouveau artist who flourished in Paris at the turn of the century. Another dog is named Hector, after Hector Guimard, the French Art Nouveau designer whose side table can be glimpsed on the platform to the far right, next to a Stickley rocker. Albert also admires the Catalan artist and architect Antoní Gaudí, but no one has been named after him so far. The dog is flanked by statuary on two of Albert's pedestals. The left is a Viennese plaster piece by an artist named Goldscheider. To the right is a French bronze of St. George. The upstairs balcony can be glimpsed through the skylight in the living room ceiling. Part of the floor was raised to create a homier feeling; the ceiling there is only ten feet above the platform, and the view is toward the main hallway.

Dining Area

The Renaissance-revival library
table serves as a dining table,
surrounded by Stickley chairs.
Horns, antlers, and skulls
decorating the area include
those of a goat and buffalo.
Albert likes the shapes.
The bronze grouping behind
the table is from the fountain
of a Hudson River Valley estate;
farther along the wall is a
bronze architectural element
from Belgium. Albert made the
iron candlesticks on the table.

Drawing Studio

Albert and Frances's drawing
studio at the top of the house
is sixty feet long. The floors
here, as in the rest of the house,
are new maple. In the far
background is one of Wendell
Castle's plastic molar chairs.
The two men have known one
another for many years as
colleagues on the faculty of the
Rochester Institute of Technology.
The strange triangular object
on the floor against the brick
wall, at left, is the top of the old
hay chute. Various small bronze
sculptures are scattered around
the mostly white studio with
its dramatic, origami-like ceiling.

James Schriber
Woodworker

A sense of familiarity settles over you as you come in and walk around James Schriber's house. Many of the furnishings look like what you might have grown up with or seen in some up-to-date, fashionable house when you were a kid. James is a woodworker in love with the fifties, forties, and earlier decades of twentieth-century design. Who can say why certain visual elements speak to us—produce a feeling of "that's me"—while others leave us unmoved? Maybe for James it has something to do with the idea of your past living in the house with you.

A great deal in James's home shows affection for the past. It is as if the angles of classic New England design, or of the flat Ohio countryside where he grew up, have given way, melted into the softer curves of domestic furnishings that began appearing in the late twenties and continued in some form through the fifties. About the only right angles in James's house are on bookshelves, storage shelves and cabinets, and a large standing screen he once made for a special exhibition.

He is particularly attracted to furniture and decorative objects that have a strong design element. Of course, much of what he collects reflects his own work—pieces with rounded edges reminiscent of Art Deco and Moderne styles. Whether it is made of exotic woods and inlays, is highly polished, or displays simple, subtle curves and is covered in milk paint, James's furniture all has a common thread. He also likes mid-century modern designs that became American classics, such as the work of Charles Eames and the Scandinavian designer Hans Wegner. He has chairs he just "came across" by each of them. As with many craftsmen's homes, James's decor is a combination of his own work, what he has discovered at flea markets and country shops (or, in one case, in an abandoned barn), and work by other designers and craftsmen.

James's father had a sheet-metal shop. James grew up in that shop, and he liked the idea that his father, in creating his own shop, had captured the pleasures of the past. He did not know what he wanted to do when he went to a small college in Vermont, but the educational experience was a catalyst that ultimately returned him to his origins. One of his teachers was a practicing architect who gave the students opportunities for hands-on experience. James realized while taking his class that it was not building houses, as such, but working with wood that called to him: He had a need to craft things. Woodworking "felt right" because he could design and build and express himself artistically in one all-encompassing activity.

His approach to his work today has both an artistic side and a business side. It is balanced among commissions, making cabinets and storage pieces, and making furniture for gallery and museum exhibitions. In this last category he displays a more eclectic interest in historic furniture than is apparent in what he has chosen for his own home. James employs from one to three people in his business, an approach that represents the smaller end of the spectrum for studio furniture makers. Most studio furniture people teach. Only a few, like James, maintain a full-time business in addition to their gallery work.

After further schooling in his craft at Boston University, James ended up in Connecticut, where he set up his own business and lived in town in a loft he converted. After some years he and Karen Ross, with whom he shares his life and his home, decided they were ready for their own house. James grew up in Dayton, surrounded

by the cornfields of southwest Ohio, and he loved the white farmhouses with their green shingled roofs. He wanted a similar look for his own home. He hired his friend and former partner, architect McKee Patterson. James and Mac had owned and run a construction firm, called Full House, that provided comprehensive services, from putting up the house to planning and installing the cabinetry. For his own house, James gave input at every step. He knew he wanted an archetypal "house" with a big front porch. The result of their collaboration was a white clapboard house sitting in a garden, with tall old trees, a lawn, and about three acres of woods. The post-and-beam porch runs around on three sides.

The heart of the house is the open living room and kitchen area. In the high-ceilinged room is a hemlock canopy of timber-frame construction. Diagonal wood brackets run from either side of the posts to the horizontal beam, forming the kind of Y-shaped support associated with country porches.

There were several reasons for installing an unusual canopy that forms a kind of roof under the ceiling. James wanted texture in a room that had mostly smoothness and not much detailing, and, as he is a wood person, wood seemed a good way to get it. The canopy echoes the design of the porch and unifies the open kitchen and living room beneath it. It also has a psychological function—it is an area both set apart and protected. With the openness all around, sitting in the room is like sitting on a porch, like being on vacation. It's not what you would usually associate with New England—not *indoors*.

The builders did everything up to the Sheetrock, and then James took over. He did all the interior work, including the Victorian-style trim around the windows, all the built-in cabinetry, and all the finishing touches. James and Karen found and salvaged many reusable items and stored them away until needed—plumbing, electrical parts, light fixtures. James knows the building trade, so he knew what he had to collect. The house was started in 1987 and took nine months to complete. Eventually, James and Karen want to put in a barn for a garage, and they might build a shop too—although James has said that he would never want a shop at home. He works at a building in town, near Karen's hairdressing salon.

Porch

On the front porch, a pair of benches James made (one painted white, the other a grayish blue) flank the double doors to the living room. He also made the table. Off to the left, on the lawn, is a pedestal-based weather vane by metal sculptor Jonathan Bonner. A wooden folk art fish sits on the porch floor.

Hallway

Stairs lead up to the second floor. Diagonally shaped frames hold tiles by ceramist Elizabeth McDonald. The floor is southern yellow pine; on it is a contemporary Oriental area rug. The stair runner is a rag rug found in pristine condition in an antique store; James had it cut to the right length and then taped. The hall chandelier is another junk-store find. On the back wall, beneath the mirror, is a wall-mounted grade-school drinking fountain that a friend found and gave to them. It is just the kind of "dated green" James admires. He calls it "functional sculpture."

Living Room, Under Canopy
left

A timber-frame wood canopy covers part of the living room and the open kitchen at the far left. Under the canopy is a couch in cherry wood and blue leather that James made. He also made the coffee table, which has a top of rose Verona marble; the black painted console table against the wall; and, on the other side of the window, a standing screen he created from Colorcore for a furniture exhibition organized by the company that makes Formica. He also made the small, boat-shaped container on the coffee table. The vase, filled with mountain laurel from their woods, was bought because James liked the art-pottery color. The candlesticks are painted glass. The pair of retro chrome-and-red-leather chairs are from the offices of the National Cash Register Company in Dayton, Ohio, James's home-town. The pillows on them are covered in a 1940s fabric Karen found, the same fabric that covers a pillow on the porch. The couch pillows are covered with Oriental-rug fabric. On the black console table is a clock by woodworker Garry Knox Bennett. Above it on the wall is a three-dimensional box by Tommy Simpson.

Living Room
right

Between the chrome-and-leather chairs is a painted wooden butler stand from the twenties and thirties that typically held an ashtray. On the back wall is a black iron woodstove from Vermont, a reproduction of an antique stove. The wall in back is decoratively protected with a sheet of galvanized corrugated barn roofing. To the left of the corrugated sheeting is a tall cabinet by woodworker Wendy Maruyama; a contemporary South American pot sits on top of it. Near the left-hand window is a chair by the Danish designer Hans Wegner. Barely visible on the other side of the couch is a cardboard box made by woodworker Tom Loeser. A curly maple candle stand that James made stands on the other side of the stove. A painted green container by furniture maker Michael Hurwitz is on top of the stand. Missy Stevens wove the rug on the floor. Two posts of the wood canopy frame the woodstove at one end of the living room. The dining area is at the far right, just beyond the kitchen.

James and Karen keep the ground floor of the house for themselves; they found they enjoyed a one-floor, open-plan living space when they had the loft in town. The second floor is for Karen's daughter Heidi, who recently graduated from college. On the top floor there is a guest room. The living room and kitchen take up most of the first floor. On the west side of the house there is a screened dining porch—a continuation of the wraparound porch. Next to it is the indoor dining room, just off the kitchen. On the other side of the kitchen is a washing-up pantry. They decided that if they were going to have an open kitchen, they would want someplace where the business end of entertaining could happen, the dirty dishes kept out of sight. Their bedroom and bath are also on the first floor, at the back of the house, facing north. There is a little balcony off the bedroom, looking out at the woods.

For James his house is an icon, as economical in its lines as a child's drawing—a simple, visually accessible, nostalgic form that can be taken in at a glance. And for him, building and furnishing the house was simply a large-scale version of making furniture.

Kitchen l e f t

James built the open kitchen, which is roofed by the wooden canopy. The almost-invisible glass doors are made visible by small red plastic pulls from the fifties, also used on the storage drawers below — James found someone who had a whole box of them. The glass-doored shelves display the couple's collection of brightly colored, simply-shaped Fiesta ware — a 1930s design that has enjoyed a considerable resurgence — as well as serving pieces by the noted American designer Russel Wright. The colored stemware is contemporary. Among the curiosities on top of the shelves are a 1940s table fan found at a flea market, two toy truck models, a sheet metal Statue of Liberty candleholder, and an aluminum and Bakelite cocktail shaker. Below the shelves is a rebuilt 1950s enamel gas stove; a chrome bread box found at a flea market is on the right. Lighting under the shelves is provided by a pair of retrieved industrial bulbs in wire cages. Opposite, the storage and work island features James's curving, bird's-eye maple countertop, which was cut to accommodate a butler's sink. The chairs, made by James, are painted white and slate-blue and have rabbeted cylindrical armrests and low stretchers that can double as footrests. The counter is used for informal meals like lunch, or for friends to chat and have a drink while dinner is being prepared under their noses. The formal dining area is to the left. At right, stairs run up behind the kitchen; the washing-up pantry is around the corner from the hallway and stairs.

Dining Room l e f t

The table in the dining room is a piece of transformable furniture James made. When the top of the bird's-eye maple table is flipped up, it forms the back of a settle, the base of which is a painted-wood and maple chest. The classic Charles Eames chair with narrow rod legs was a find. The nail head–trimmed chairs on the other side of the table have blue Naugahyde seats. In the left-hand corner is an old cream separator that looks like an antique Chinese artifact. On the table, on either side of the vase, are candleholders by Jonathan Bonner. The screened porch is off to the left.

Screened Porch a b o v e

Serving as a summer dining room, the porch can comfortably accommodate about six people. The table has a tubular chrome base with an oval top rimmed in aluminum. To make it larger, James had a piece of glass cut in an oval that extends about ten inches beyond the original table beneath. Cantilevered metal chairs are among a number of pieces in the house that have a retro look. The floor of the dining porch is painted the same grayish blue as the chairs. An old wicker-covered vacuum bottle sits on a table.

Bedroom   James made the bed, which is cherry veneer with narrow strips of ebony inlay, and the pair of matching bedside night tables. The unmatched pair of bedside lamps are by the furniture maker Garry Knox Bennett. The brightly colored monoprint above the bed is by Todd McKee, a painter, papermaker, and occasional ceramist. The strange, white, dinosaur-size bone in the corner is actually a clock made by woodworker Ed Zucca; it's called *Great-Great-Grandfather's Clock*. The muslin curtains at the windows are hung from stripped tree branches tied into the space. The French door leads out to a small balcony that overlooks the woods.

Thomas Mann

Jewelry Maker

To understand Thomas Mann's home, you have to look at his handcrafted jewelry. To understand his jewelry, you have to look at his background.

Tom, who grew up in Pennsylvania, had two interests early on. He received his undergraduate degree in performing arts, with an emphasis on set design. But he had been making jewelry since high school, learning the basics of the craft from a metalsmith who had a shop in town. He paid part of his way through college making silver bangles and such. After graduation, he chose full-time jewelry making over Broadway. Over more than two decades, he has been showing and selling his work in galleries and at craft fairs around the country, and more recently in his own gallery in New Orleans.

Thomas's jewelry could be described as a collection of props that have been assembled for something about to happen, or even as a stage on which the curtain has begun to part. He himself describes his work as theatrical. He calls his pieces "visual stories," in which the designer, the wearer, and the observer are all involved in the way each exercises his or her imagination on the work.

The pieces are an amalgam of nonprecious metals and found objects assembled in an almost willy-nilly way that gives the work spontaneity, as if the design of each piece depended on what the maker's hand grasped next from the worktable—like an ad-libbed scene. His house has the same feeling: it is very much in flux, nothing is nailed down, the decorating is fluid, and everything can be easily changed.

Thomas gathers jewelry components nationwide, from New York City's Canal Street—that mecca of odd parts—to a store in Florida that sells Kennedy Space Center surplus. He fills in the missing pieces with discontinued jewelry parts from Providence, Rhode Island, and what he digs up in flea markets around the country.

Many of his jewelry designs involve what he regards as two opposing elements, a style he gives the split name "Techno-Romantic." On the one hand there are the screws, nuts, bolts, washers, perforated sheet metal, plastics, resins, discarded jewelry findings, and other industrial stuff. These souvenirs of our technical age are combined with images from old postcards or photographs. These are invariably of young women—wistful, dreamy, coy girls with out-of-date hairdos—gazing through the base metal that surrounds them.

In addition to his more flamboyant designs, he also creates limited production pieces. He employs twenty to thirty people in a studio in another part of town, where he also has a gallery for exhibitions, and a shop. Since 1989 he has been giving workshops around the country to craftsmen and various organizations on how to run an efficient craft business while still doing what you want to do. One of the basic principles of his successful operation is the separation of the work into different lines—a less expensive line that is manufactured, and the more expressive, one-of-a-kind pieces.

Tom also makes furniture, mostly for his own use, that looks like larger versions of his pins. Or, put the other way round, if the chairs and tables were shrunk, you could wear them on your suit and people in the know would say, "Isn't that a piece by Tom Mann?"

Living Room The room is divided by a brick chimneypiece with a gas fireplace. Ceramic pieces hanging above the fireplace are by craftsmen friends. Tom made the glass-topped steel table and the chair in the foreground, which has a perforated aluminum seat and mahogany back. The chair to the left is by a craftsman friend, Ries Niemi; the chair on the far side of the table is by another craftsman, Herman Caro. (The entire room, like the rest of the house, is filled with pieces by craftsmen Tom knows.) The wall on the right is dressed up with a pressed-board panel stained green, and the TV cabinet beyond it, in the corner, is topped by a glass-and-cement lamp. French doors at the far end lead to the guest room and bath. The shelf, made of steel, is suspended from cables above the French doors. Sculptures by Tom sit on either side. The ceiling is twelve feet high at the roof ridge.

Tom had visited New Orleans for years; eventually he began spending half the year there. Finally, a few years ago, he decided to settle in New Orleans. He opened his gallery there and bought this house. He is a bachelor, and New Orleans fits right in with his lifestyle; it is a lively town.

He lives near the water in an old part of New Orleans called the Irish Channel. The house dates from about 1880 and is typical of the area—delightfully seedy in a Tennessee Williams sort of way. The houses are close together and near the street, and the area has antique shops and restaurants that give it a European feeling. His house, like many in the area, is called a shotgun because of its shape. Under old New Orleans laws, property tax was levied on a building's frontage and on its number of windows and rooms. Boxcar-shaped buildings became popular, and to get around the levy on frontage only the back half of many houses had second floors. This arrangement is called a camelback.

The house has Delta blue clapboard with white trim. Its main entrance is on the side, through a small yard with some flowers and a Japanese plum tree. The side porch, where the entrance door is located, has an assortment of chairs and benches and some plants. This house is much more focused on the interior than some of the others in this book, where the surroundings and gardens have been given more attention.

Although long and narrow—just one room wide—the house does not have a cramped feeling because it has high ceilings, twelve feet at the highest point, and six-foot-high windows. Tom has trouble finding window coverings for them, but they let a great deal of light into the open spaces.

You enter by walking into the dining room. The living room is to the right, a double parlor divided by the freestanding brick fireplace in the middle of the room. Beyond it, at the front of the house where it faces the street, is a guest room and bath behind glass doors covered with blinds. If you turn to the left, you are facing the kitchen door and the stairs up to the second-floor bedrooms. Out beyond the kitchen Tom plans to build a deck.

Living Room f a r l e f t

Tom made the couch about twenty years ago out of plywood. It is now painted yellow and scattered with pillows, including several made of silk hand-painted by a friend. The sculpture on the shelf is by Tom. The wire man on the stand is one of a number of steel sculptures Tom has by a craftsman friend, John Martini.

Living Room l e f t

The wooden table and chair Tom made and painted is reminiscent of his jewelry; it contains miscellaneous objects under the glass tabletop that have been painted white; under the chair seat are some rocks from Maine. The chair back is made of wire nailed to the sides. The iron standing candlesticks flanking the creation were made by a New Mexico craftsman, Keith Mueller. The two photographs above the table were taken by Steven John Phillips, with whom Tom sometimes works (he uses Phillips's images in his jewelry).

Dining Room

Tom made the dining room table and chairs. The floor, like all the others in the house, is yellow pine. He also made the standing light in the corner; light radiates from behind perforated screening, where the lamp is supported by the horizontal rod that rests on the perpendicular walls. He made the lighting arrangement over the table as well; it is simply bulbs inside conical reflectors suspended from electrical wire. The zigzag light going up the center of the chimney piece is neon tubing. He made the white box on the floor; it's under a friend's painting. Through the doorway the kitchen stairs are visible; they lead up to the second-floor bedrooms.

Dining Room

The piece hanging on the wall next to the fireplace—called *908*—is a kind of accidental sculpture: Tom found it after it fell off a New Orleans bus. The pasteboard cutouts on the hearth—a baby, a dog, and a cat—are actually photographs laminated on cardboard. Tom refers to them as his "low-maintenance family."

The table is made of steel, as are the chairs. The legs are steel tubing; the backs of the chairs are made from half-inch square steel rods. Under the glass top of the table is a bed of pea gravel on which Tom has arranged railroad scrap—rusted strips that have peeled off the rails. He likes rusted metal and found these samples around local railroad tracks. Like some other craftsmen, Tom likes to salvage urban throwaways.

Kitchen

The antique cooking stove, probably from the thirties, was bought in New Orleans but is called Detroit Jewel. Under the brand name is a slogan: "They bake better." The brick chimneypiece (the back of the dining room fireplace) is covered with kitchen gadgets and other odds and ends Tom has picked up at flea markets. He is thinking of eventually covering the brick completely with hanging items. The wire "face" chair next to the stove is a counterpart to a chair in the living room. The cartage box, hanging on the wall next to the stove, was bought to use as an herb cupboard.

Kitchen

The old baking cabinet under the stairs belonged to Tom's grandmother; he has memories of baking Christmas cookies with her. It stands alongside a modern cabinet that holds his coffeemaker—he is a coffee aficionado. Next to the stairs is a Cajun-style rocking chair. The rag rug on the kitchen floor is by craftsman Sara Hotchkiss. The red glow at the top of the stairs, which lead up to the bedrooms, is from a neon light.

Exterior

The entrance is through a small fenced-off yard and up a couple of steps to a flower-bordered porch and a casual collection of seating, most of which Tom found at flea markets.

Bedroom

On the second floor is Tom's bedroom, a second bedroom, a bath, and a laundry area. Tom's interest in collage is exercised in a different way in this room — textile patterns played off one another. The Native American rugs on the bed and daybed, from New Mexico, are set against a quilt and patterned pillows. Another set of linear patterns appears in the Swedish rag rugs on the floor. The tall paper lamp next to the bed is a design by the late sculptor Isamu Noguchi. The Cajun twig table next to the lamp is one of several in the house. Tom does much of his drawing while sitting on the daybed.

Tom's creations are in all of the rooms — if not furniture, then lighting fixtures, or assemblages, or something he found and arranged. And any of the pieces are likely to change when you turn your back. He is always trying things out to see how they will work. If the decor has a fixed characteristic, it is that virtually every room holds dozens, maybe hundreds of pieces by craftsmen Tom knows. Tom is gregarious and has done a great deal of trading at craft fairs: his jewelry for other people's work. The items he has by other craftsmen range from ceramic pots to metal furniture and everything in between. He knows what all the craftsmen do and where they live, their backgrounds, and what is going on in their lives today — it's part of the fabric of his life to have all these connections. He says that when he comes home at night he feels as if he is coming home to friends, surrounded as he is by their work. His things are also a journal of his experiences and friendships. I think everybody, to a certain degree, looks at the things they own or have collected as markers in time.

Tom is goal-oriented and energetic and thrives on a great deal of activity. The idea of having a home is a new one for him. He is discovering for the first time the joys of surrounding himself with his own unique designs and creating a place all his own.

Roy Superior
Woodworker

Mara Superior
Ceramist

Roy and Mara Superior's white clapboard house is the quintessential rural New England home. It sits on a village street in a hill town with not much more than a post office and a grocery store. The impression of America at home grows when you open their front door and walk into an atmosphere so cheerful and welcoming you sniff for the roast in the oven and the apple pie cooling on the windowsill.

They bought the house in the year of its 150th anniversary. It was built in 1828 in the country Greek Revival style and had not been particularly well loved by its previous owners—twenty in less than forty years.

Roy and Mara moved to western Massachusetts from Connecticut because Roy had accepted a teaching job. They were looking for something affordable that also offered studio space, although they would have settled for a good shell they could work on and adapt. But when they found a house with an attached barn, Roy saw "studio" written all over it. And Mara liked the house because it was on the street, and you could hear the cars going by—she is originally from New York City.

Roy and Mara met in the early seventies when he was teaching art at the Hartford Art School, University of Hartford, where Mara was a student. They fell in love, married, and moved to Massachusetts in the mid seventies, when Roy took a job as an associate professor of art at Hampshire College in Amherst.

They had figured it would take about three months to fix up the two-story house—tearing down walls, opening ceilings, stripping wallpaper and plaster, and moving and removing doors. By the time they finished, after three *years* of work, they had redefined the interior space and developed quite a bit of sweat equity in their property. They also made a couple of discoveries along the way—they expected the usual mouse nests and were delighted by the 1875 newspaper clipping about a balloon flight to Boston, but they were really excited when they found a deteriorated brick wall and a handsome hearthstone. That spot, with the brick wall returned to respectability through the efforts of Roy and a friend, is now glorified by the imposing old iron stove that came with the house and goes by the brand name of Quaker Social.

Visually and symbolically, the stove serves as the heart of the house, the center around which life flows—the kitchen around it; the sitting room, lined with books, just in front of it, with Roy's music stand in the corner (he plays a mean clarinet); the more formal dining room beyond that; a little office off to the side; and Roy's studio behind the house. Within the flow of the semiopen plan and its traffic patterns, the objects Roy and Mara have collected are directional signals and signs, reminders of the life lived there and the art of its owners.

Kitchen, Woodstove Area

Just inside the sitting room at the far end is a music stand and stool Roy made; he is a traditional jazz clarinetist. Some old copper pots and pans hang on the brick wall behind the woodstove, which came with the house. Mara's drawing on ceramic of a woodstove is to the right of the stovepipe. The top shelf of the stove is dotted with small lidded bowls, each covered with a broody china bird. Among the baskets hanging from the ceiling are several made locally. The floor is Massachusetts pine with butternut filler between the pine boards, which are screwed down and topped with walnut pegs. The French doors behind the kitchen table lead out to a deck and Roy's studio.

Sitting Room   l e f t

The fireplace, fitted out with an 1820 Franklin stove, is on the other side of the dining room wall. Roy made the pine mantel, on top of which sits a bowl by Mara, a miniature topiary tree made locally, a small antique globe, and a pair of little wooden shoes. There is also a small wooden house, which is actually a jewelry box, with wooden smoke coming out of its chimney. Roy also made the myrtle-wood candle box on the wall; Mara made the ceramic match holder beneath it. An old sampler hangs above the mantel. The green glass shades are store-bought. The tall cupboard against the wall to the right is a TV cabinet; Roy made it and finished it with a graining effect he calls "faux bone." The molding was made by hand with antique planes. In the area behind the wall against which the cabinet rests is a small office and the first-floor bath. The drawing to the right of the cabinet is Roy's pen-and-ink self-portrait. The large porcelain vase on top of the mantel is Mara's *Enchanted Wood*. On the wall to the left of the mantel are, in order of descent, a slab-built porcelain low relief by Mara entitled *The Hearth*, an antique print of birds, and a portrait plate Mara made. The ladder-back chair in the foreground was obtained at a local auction.

Sitting Room

Roy made the maple and tiger-maple cupboard for the corner of the living room next to the open entry to the kitchen to hold Mara's platters, teapots, and other serving pieces. It is decorated with bone inlay and purpleheart wood hearts. Alongside the cupboard are another of Mara's cow plates, a framed reproduction of an Audubon swan painting, and two dolls made by craftsman Tracey Gallup. The basket is topped with a rooster carved by Roy. In the corner of the sofa, leaning against other pillows, lies a stuffed fabric trout. The door at the far right leads out from the kitchen to the driveway.

In the early seventies, before he had "discovered" wood, both Roy and I were teaching at the Hartford Art School. One day he visited my studio and saw my work and my tools (Roy loves tools). He was primed to start something new, and woodworking—making things with his hands, creating something substantial he could walk around—seemed like an ideal medium in which to express himself, his sense of humor, and his sensibilities. One of his projects in wood was the dining room table. The eight-foot-long table takes up most of the dining room, and is made of English oak. He kept the wavy edge of the bark, as if the table were his tribute to the natural line of the tree.

It is a surprise to some people when they look at Roy's work to learn that he studied, taught, and spent many years working in mediums other than wood. He was trained in the graphic arts—drawing, painting, illustration, printmaking—but he fell in love with wood. His kinetic, Rube Goldbergian sculptures are carefully carved and joined, models of a zany and whimsical world. Verbal and visual puns are usually the vehicle for his satirical bent—one example is his *Metropolitan Hiawatha*, a small canoe on wheels that sits on the dining room table.

He also likes to create visual expressions of his concepts, with a bittersweet humor—a bicycle that goes only in circles, a miniature ladder-back chair on snowshoes. He makes ever-more-elaborate contraptions whose purposes are revealed through systems of levers, gears, cranks, and pulleys that set the "machines" into coordinated motion. It was not that great a jump from furniture to his creations: the furniture is just the quieter, functional side of his work, while the sculptures are a less tame expression of himself.

Mara's move from one medium to another was more gradual than Roy's. She earned her undergraduate degree in fine arts, with a major in painting. But she had always been interested in folk pottery—Staffordshire pots and other pottery of its kind. When she and Roy moved to Massachusetts, she began a master's degree program at the University of Massachusetts at Amherst and, as part of the program, studied ceramics. She turned to clay, finally settling on high-fired porcelain as her special medium, because it allowed her to work three-dimensionally as well as to draw and paint pictures.

Dining Room　l e f t

The banquet-size English oak dining table is eight feet long and four feet wide. The antique chairs were bought at a local auction. Roy made the open cupboard to display Mara's ceramics. *Metropolitan Hiawatha* sits on an antique embroidered linen runner. The walnut and apple-wood settle under the stairs is also from Roy's workbench. Above it is a collection of antique calling cards in a frame Roy made; he also made the frames for the animal prints and miscellaneous collections hanging on the stairwell wall. The stair and the first floor are original to the house. The entry foyer (not seen) is just off the right.

Kitchen, Detail　a b o v e

The shelves next to the refrigerator hold miscellaneous collected items and Mara's work from the last ten years— items for which she holds a special affection. Among the few things she did not make are a pitcher in the shape of a dog, a butter plate cover in the form of the house, and some lovely old china cups hanging from the cup hooks. Alongside the shelves, Roy's cutting board hangs on the wall, as well as his salad servers, flanking the light switch. The double-bowled wooden utensil below the cutting board is an African spoon.

77

Foyer, Detail

Angler's Shrine, by the front door, is Roy's altar to two of the enlightened souls of fishing—Izaak Walton and Charles Cotton; there are little statues of each inside the box. The weather vane on top shows a man fishing. (Come spring, fishing figures prominently in Roy's life.) Roy, who loves puns, carved the yew-wood cane in the corner with a devil's head, and cut into the shaft the words "Yew Old Devil." The porcelain plate to the left of the "shrine" is Mara's depiction of a cow, entitled *Cow;* to the right of the fishermen's memorial is Roy's dry-brush watercolor of a cow. When Mara first came up to New England from the "big city," she found cows very exotic.

Foyer, Detail

On the other side of the front door is a setting that includes *Wild Side*, a bowl by Mara (it has a zebra on the front) sitting on a small bird's-eye and tiger-maple table made by Roy. The chair sculpture above it is also Roy's, it is called *Terrible Twos* and refers to the exhausting energy of small children. The small Shaker-style chair hanging above the other two has springs in its legs. The muslin curtains are held back with wooden birds carved and painted by Roy. The collection of straw hats — Amish, Italian, and Chinese — are wearable.

Jewelry

All these pieces were made by Roy for Mara out of ebony and bone, most for a special occasion such as a gift-giving holiday or a birthday. Some of the figures have articulated arms, such as the mermaid pendant suspended from a necklace, and the angel, a 1988 valentine gift, which bears a carved ribbon with the words "True Love." The moon is saying, in Latin, "Love is like the moon: it comes and goes." A cow, a bucolic emblem in the Superior catalog of meanings, is in the upper right-hand corner. The ubiquitous Superior fish is on the lower right. The dog in the upper left-hand corner is entitled B*itch on Wheels.*

Kitchen Table, Detail

For a place setting on a blue and white jacquard tablecloth, Mara laid out old coin-silver spoons and a bone-handled knife and fork. They flank a trout bowl and plate made by Mara.

Mara's witty forms—exuberant teapots, plump vases—often look as though she had drawn them quickly in the air. And the images with which she decorates them are more than just nostalgic—they call to mind a time when the world could be rendered in unselfconscious lines, like a child's drawing. Mara draws and paints the things that make up her life, symbols of rural serenity like houses, gardens, teapots, and fish. And you can tell Mara's work at a glance—you would never mistake it for anyone else's.

The fish is practically Roy's personal logo. He is very enthusiastic about fly-fishing, to an extent that he would be tempted by an offer to be a fly-fishing guide. A houseboat studio might be a good solution.

One of the handy things about being a craftsman is that a good eye and a well-trained hand go a long way toward easing a tight budget. The furniture in their house that Roy did not make himself, he and Mara picked up at country auctions where they were looking for simple pieces. A number of the basics of the house—doors, a pedestal sink, lighting fixtures—were salvaged from various sources.

When Roy and Mara can't afford something they need (and they have a never-ending list) they often make it instead. They prefer to collect things that actually function—baskets, straw hats, some china and flatware, and ephemera like calling cards. Their home is filled with their finds, with what they have made professionally, and with what they have created for one another. In this sense, it is an homage to their spirit and mutual affection.

Portrait | Roy and Mara pose in front of the woodstove with their spaniel, Oliver.

Wendell Castle
Woodworker

Nancy Jurs
Ceramist

Wendell Castle and Nancy Jurs live in a large, old house in upstate New York. It is square and solid-looking, with a sweeping driveway that ends in an imposing porte cochere, and looks more like the home of a successful burgher than two craftsmen.

In fact, the house was built in 1905 by a family of well-off farmers and mill owners, who named it Oakwood. It had all the amenities of the day, including large bedrooms (each with its own bath) and multiple fireplaces. It was this, along with the fact that the house was in move-in condition, as the real estate ads say, that persuaded the couple to buy it. They could live in it while they renovated it. With the busy lives these two lead, that must have seemed like a good idea.

They bought the house in 1978 and have been shifting things around ever since. The house is in constant flux; something is always being changed or redone. You come one time and see that the bedroom has been turned into a sewing room, or vice versa, and the next time it is something else. For craftsmen, trying out creative ideas is essential, and anything is fair game—including, and even especially, their homes.

Recently the couple decided they would like to have the greenhouse—which came with the original property—connected to the house. That meant building an addition. As is so often the case with remodeling, they got a bigger bite of reality than they had expected and went from something practical to something major. Because—as it turns out—when you add a room, you have to put in a basement. And then, since you are going to all that expense and trouble, you might as well put on a second floor.

The first floor of the addition is the new kitchen. The old kitchen was pleasant and old-fashioned, and was built in a more leisurely age when anyone who lived in a big house had help. The new kitchen is to be much larger and greatly modernized. The pantry, which lies between the old kitchen and the dining room, has already been contemporized, and the kitchen now includes an eat-in area. Before, all the eating was done in the formal dining room. This is a house that sees the comings and goings of many people—family (Nancy's mother and son drop by often), friends, and Wendell's employees. You go for lunch and you end up eating dinner with four other people who dropped by serendipitously.

The second floor of the addition, which I think was about two hours old when we came to visit, is the new master bedroom. It is full of Wendell's furniture and Nancy's ceramics, as is the rest of the house.

There are some aspects of the house they have left alone. The big center hall is as it always has been, even down to the graceful old stair railing. The moldings and trim in the living room and dining room are still in place. When they first moved in, they painted the living room mantel and window trim silver.

Their renovation of the house is obviously not an attempt to restore a 1905 dwelling to its original appearance. Since Wendell is a furniture maker, the house has the look of his work: virtually all the furniture and built-ins are what he or his employees made in his studio across town. For the most part his furniture and Nancy's ceramics were made over the last ten years. They are interspersed with older pieces.

Outdoors | The house is surrounded by formal, parklike grounds. An expansive lawn shaded by many beautiful, old trees is enlivened by banks and beds of flowers and flowering shrubs. Several of Nancy's sculptures stand on the lawn.

Outdoors | Wendell's molar chairs on an expanse of lawn.

Detail | Some of Nancy's larger clay sculptures, her Southwest series, stand in a corner of the dining room before a lithograph by Alphonse Mucha. Next to them, on top of the radiator, are clay studies for larger pieces. The door at right leads to the center hall.

Dining Room | Wendell's dining table is made of holly and purpleheart wood with a curving black leather edge. Inlaid into the top is a series of dots; if they were connected they would spell out "Never complain, never explain." The small pear wood and ebony cabinet on the stand to the left of the window was made to hold liquor. The mirrored pedestals on the other side of the window were designed by Wendell and Nancy and hold Nancy's ceramic pieces. More work by Nancy, which has a patina applied by torch, sits on the mantel near the clock made by Wendell. The chairs around the dining table are made of purpleheart wood and covered in black leather. The flowers in front of the window sit in one of Nancy's "blouse" vessels; a porcelain bowl in the center of the dining table, from her "wedding gift" series, holds fruit.

Wendell is a boy from Kansas who established an international reputation as a studio furniture maker. He showed an early interest in working with wood, and as a youngster he carved all kinds of things and was constantly drawing. He is a master of technique who is fascinated by the inherent beauty of his material. Over the years he has maintained his experimental and sculptural style; recently he has begun to paint his pieces.

His first work, after he began teaching furniture design and furniture making at Rochester Institute of Technology's School for American Craftsmen, was the stacked, laminated, carved furniture that put him on the map. After about a decade of increasing public awareness, he began to explore other solutions to furniture making, other modes of expression within the field of woodworking. He went through a number of stages, including a brief flirtation with molded plastic chairs he called "molar chairs," probably because they look like back teeth. He now has some of them in the garden and greenhouse. He built trompe l'oeil furniture for a while, and then ranged far and wide through styles and periods until his work began to evolve as a unique and personal statement.

Nancy's work is also experimental and varied. She has worked in contained "series," as she calls them, many of them centered on women's issues. She went to R.I.T. and became a ceramist. Her work includes a variety of forms, from conventional vessels to what one reviewer called "women disguised as clothing," to chimney-pot shapes, to large-scale sculptures in clay. She particularly enjoys building monumental works in clay; some of these can be found throughout the house and garden. She created a thirteen-foot-high abstract sculpture for a building at the University of Rochester, and was one of the artists selected to do a sculpture for the Rochester airport. She exhibits her work at galleries around the country. Of late, she has been working in raku, and most recently she has been applying a patina to already fired pots with a torch, demonstrating a skill and daring that characterizes much of her work.

Wendell and Nancy have each done a great deal of exploring in their work, and this shows in their house. It may be that both the house and their work will continue to represent the inevitable changes in their outlooks and experience.

Living Room   l e f t

The mantel of this fireplace was painted silver by the couple when they moved in, as was the window trim; both are original to the house. Moldings here and in the hall and dining room are also originals. The living room offers a rich array of reflections and patterns, seen in the Oriental rug, the old paisley shawl draped over the arm of a sofa, and Wendell's unusual coffee table with its painted "saddlebag" base. Wendell and Nancy constructed the leather couches in the mid seventies. Wendell's guitar rests against patterned throw pillows on the couch. Ceramic pieces on the mantel are by David Gilhooly. The clock on the right side of the mantel is Wendell's, as is the little bronze chair sitting on the coffee table. Over the mantel is a drawing of the Castle family by Bob Clarke. Hydrangeas in the foreground are from the garden.

Center Hall   a b o v e

The large center hall has remained as it was when the couple bought the house. Many elements, including the graceful stair railing, are original. The door under the stairs leads to a downstairs bath; the door in the back leads to the new kitchen area. The stairwell is lined with Nancy's ceramic pieces. The console table against the side of the stairs is Wendell's; the bowl on top of it is by Dorothy Baker. Nancy is sitting on the lower stairs.

Pantry far left

The updated pantry between
the old kitchen and the dining
room has built-in cabinetry made
and designed by Jim Hill. The
cabinet in the foreground has an
opening in the shape of spoons;
the cabinet just beyond it has
drawer pulls in the shape of little
chairs. The pyramidal lighting
fixture on top of the cabinet is
metal with green coloring and
was made by Wendell. More of
Nancy's ceramic pieces sit in
various places in the pantry.

Detail left

More built-in cabinetry made
by Jim Hill. The faux tile effect on
the wall and ceiling was done by
Nancy, who attached quarter-inch
masonite panels to the wall
and sponged and rubbed them
to achieve the look of an old
building. The airbrush painting is
by Marlene Scott. The bowl on
the counter is by William Sellers,
from the fifties.

Master Bedroom

Wendell relaxes in his new bedroom amid some of his work: a rocker covered in leather with an ebonized mahogany structure, a sculptural cabinet meant to call up the idea of cows, and another mantel clock. The fireplace was efficiently planned: the cabinets on either side hold firewood and a TV and Stereo. The fireplace surround is colored metal. The niche holds work by Nancy and others. The painting above the fireplace is by Kathy Calderwood. The almost imperceptible door to the right of the fireplace arrangement is a closet. Behind Wendell is a window overlooking the greenhouse.

A vaulted ceiling soars over the new master bedroom, on the second floor of the addition connecting the greenhouse with the house. The niche set just below the ceiling holds work by Nancy, and at the far right is a piece by Wendell that looks like ceramic but is actually made of painted wood. Above the bed are two prints by Art Nouveau artist and designer Alphonse Mucha, aptly titled *Morning* and *Evening*. Sophie, the stuffed bear on the bed, has won a permanent home there. A dictionary stand in maple, made by Wendell, is in the foreground.

Leo Sewell
Mixed Media

What society throws out, Leo Sewell rescues and crafts into sculpture. If he has 100,000 little parts of things stored away in his place it wouldn't surprise me in the least. Plastics of all kinds, metal scraps, wooden scraps, every conceivable piece of junk ever thrown out—these are the foundations of Leo's sculpture. He was featured in Ripley's "Believe It or Not" column, and his work is in the Ripley museums. Leo has also used all kinds of things to make much of his household furniture.

Leo lives in Philadelphia, and says he settled there because it is "a great place for junk." Clearly this is not what every American is looking for in their hometown. In 1978 he bought a three-story brick carriage house with a gambrel roof and a backyard and fixed it up. It is about a century old and sits on a narrow street, almost an alleyway. Later he acquired an old sign-painting shop directly next door, which he uses for his studio, and turned the roof of the shop into a large terrace that leads into the dining room of his house. He and his wife, Barbara, met when he was fixing up the house. A mutual friend, sure they would hit it off, told Barbara she should go over to Leo's and see if he would rent her a room. The friend was right.

Serendipity—finding great things or experiences when you do not expect to—has always been a part of Leo's life. As a kid in Annapolis, Maryland, he scouted the Navy dump and found all kinds of "whiz-bang" things. "Every week was like Christmas," he says of his childhood. But his parents told him he could not have all that junk just lying around—he would have to make something with it. Leo's father, a teacher, was obsessed with finding things and restoring them. He had a home workshop where he refinished furniture and made simple things from objects he had salvaged. It sounds like the apple did not fall far from the tree.

Leo got his master's degree in art history from the University of Delaware. The subject of his thesis was, appropriately, "Use of the Found Object in Dada and Surrealism." His vocation was inevitable. Leo's attitude toward his finished artistic product is a little different from most artists', in that he makes sculpture in order to continue his obsession with finding things: leftover, discarded, man-made artifacts. When you think about it, many craftsmen are in love with their materials. Leo's just happens to be junk.

Leo's aesthetic fits his philosophy, a belief in recycling, reusing, and using up—not choking the world with more waste. If you take ivory and ebony and gold and put them together, you can make something stupid and still have it look great because of the materials. Leo prefers to make something useful and attractive out of discards. Making junk look great takes real talent.

Living Room One of Leo's sculptures, entitled *Miscellaneous* (a phonetic pun), sits on a velvet-cushioned Gothic church bench. Near her left foot is a Leo junk dachshund; a Leo boxer sits nearby. The grandfather clock is made from cut-up Ouija boards, wooden beads, children's blocks, rulers, and other oddments, in a classic open-pediment style. The finial is a pot-metal statuette of a cheerleader holding pom-poms in each hand. The clock face is from a local beverage vendor's establishment. The wing chair next to the clock, and the Chippendale-style straight-back chair opposite, are both upholstered in patches. Above the wing chair is one of Barbara's quilts. In the corner is a figural sculpture Leo made out of light bulbs. The giant insect larva–like object hanging from the stairs is actually a compacted stack of 1929 pharmacy receipts—Leo finds a use for everything! On the other side of the circular metal stairs that lead up to Barbara and Leo's bedroom is an old-fashioned washing machine used here just for its decorative value. The rocker in the foreground was a trash find; the green stained chest nearby serves as a coffee table. On top of it is a wooden puzzle Leo made using photographs of Abby and her schoolmates. The rug in the foreground is contemporary Iranian; the one in the background at right, also contemporary, is from Afghanistan. Next to the wing chair, on an old Philadelphia ballot box, sits a miniature tyrannosaurus that Leo made. In a corner, under the globe, is a smoking cabinet Leo's father made; its door pulls are smoking-pipe halves. On the chest of drawers under the window is an old shoe-making mold.

I think Leo believes that you should make the most out of everything that is lying around in the world, or "eating everything on your plate." But for him it is more than just using up, reusing, making something useful. He takes an extra step and transforms trash into wonderful pieces of art. It is not enough for him to say, "Well, now I found a use for all this junk so I feel better about myself." He wants to make something beautiful.

But Leo does love the junk itself. He used to go out religiously, three times a week, with a pickup truck to different dumps, Salvation Army centers, factories, and specialty junk dealers (one a guy who has thousands of license plates). After twenty-five years of this, he has a whole network of places and contacts. Leo likes the daily interaction with people and the adventure of finding things in a big city.

In his studio Leo has things stored up to the ceiling —corridors full of stuff—but it is very neat. When you have that much stuff, you have to organize it. Barbara is actively involved in her husband's work and does most of the organizing for the consumption of junk. She has a computer in her newly constructed office in their home, where she keeps track of the many church sales, yard sales, and flea markets in the area, as well as works on the selection and placement of Leo's objects in the house. She also keeps her hand in the real estate business, an earlier full-time career, and occasionally makes quilts.

Leo's sculptures have a wooden core. He screws and nails and bolts things onto the core, shaping the piece as he goes along and building it up bit by bit. He packs everything so tightly you see only the things immediately behind the outer layer. His furniture includes a small buffet-bar, separating the kitchen from the dining room, made of Pennsylvania license plates. A grandfather clock in the living room is made partly from cut-up Ouija boards, wooden beads, and children's blocks. In addition to the furniture, some of his sculptures can be found in the house. A life-size assembled woman sits on a real pew in the living room. (Leo likes to make things life-size.)

The house is compact. The first floor has a long hall running from the front door to the arched back door, leading to the backyard. Daughter Abby's room is tucked into one corner, and Barbara's office is next door. The third floor, the old hayloft, is Barbara and Leo's bedroom. It has an enormous skylight and is just as filled with oddities as is the rest of the house.

Dining Room

An assortment of chairs surrounds the dining table. The chair at the head of the table was restored by Leo's father. The container on the table is by Roseville, an early twentieth-century pottery company. The sideboard against the wall is made from skis, poised vertically, with dartboards and a cribbage board at the top and colored rulers below, all applied to an old jelly cupboard. The floor-standing wine cooler to the left is composed of various metal containers. The painting, from 1946, was purchased at a yard sale. The chandelier above the dining table is made partly from the innards of a washing machine.

Kitchen

Part of the open space on the second floor, the kitchen is just beyond the top of the stairs and the dictionary stand. The freestanding buffet separating the kitchen from the dining area is made of old Pennsylvania license plates. Leo made the open cupboard next to the refrigerator; the base has an old icebox door. The thick countertop is from a bowling alley and supports a collection of bowls. On top of the refrigerator, which displays one of Abby's drawings, is a little house made of rulers. On the wall next to the refrigerator is a painting of cows by an anonymous woman, and a framed collection of old Philadelphia mummer's ribbons. The half-wall partition at the lower right has a glass panel, behind which Leo has arranged colorful patches of dryer lint.

The second floor—the filling in the sandwich—is where most of the daytime living takes place. The open space is sectioned off into a kitchen, dining area, living room, and bathroom. A curving metal staircase in the living room leads up to the hayloft/master bedroom. High arched windows in the rooms look out on the street and the backyard. A door in the dining room leads out to the second-floor terrace.

If you look carefully at the objects Leo has made, and see them without preconceptions, you see them differently, as pieces of art. A hard second look, and the objects transcend the material from which they are made and you see the concepts and associations behind them.

What Leo does is integrate ideas that give joy and delight, without all the baggage of authority, the biases and prejudices of the high-powered art establishment. With a number of craftsmen, I have noticed the intoxication of dealing directly with their heart and intuitions, of making something with no encumbrances or restraints. It does something marvelous to your spirit if you can sustain that direct connection, and Leo has managed to raise it to an art form.

Bedroom The master bedroom on the top floor is lit by arched windows and a skylight. The bed in the center is covered with a quilt Barbara made from clothing scraps. The rug beside the bed was bought at a charity auction; it depicts George Washington entering heaven. Family mittens and gloves hanging on the clothesline are there because Barbara and Leo like the way they look. Sometimes they hang T-shirts as well, or whatever strikes their fancy. The laths covering the ceiling were found and nailed over Styrofoam insulation, which was also retrieved. The cedar chest at the head of the bed was another discovery, as was the lamp on it, which was picked up in a trash bin. At the foot of the bed is a braided rug made by Leo and Barbara from old neckties. A very strange rug in the room (not seen) was braided from plastic bread bags. The stuffed owl in the rafters was a gift. The spiral object silhouetted against the window is one of Leo's favorite creations: a snake made from the bottom halves of forty flatirons.

Wall, Detail The wall display includes an actual window with old glass negatives fitted out by Leo. The wooden box on the left holds tooth samples from a dentist's office, and supports two stuffed birds intended for a lady's hat, and a framed luna moth—one of the few things Leo did not possess as a child, although he did collect moths. Below the barometer on the right is a plaque that reads "mid-life crisis." That hole in the wall is not what it seems—it is a *photograph* of a hole in the wall.

Bathroom It is a wonder the household can brush their teeth in the morning with all the arrangements in the bathrooms. The second-floor bathroom is just on the other side of the kitchen, looking toward the dining room. Reflected in the medicine chest mirror are various religious finds of Leo's that are mounted on the opposite wall. The photographs left of the medicine chest include one of the Philadelphia Museum of Art and one of a Hollywood movie star. In the upstairs bathroom, photographs, drawings, stitchery pieces, and an oil painting of palm trees surround a giant eyeball, making it difficult to take a shower.

Studio   l e f t

Leo stands in his workshop,
where the uncountable
numbers of discards and finds
are neatly arranged in drawers,
cases, and boxes and on
shelves right up to the ceiling.
The round pedestal supporting
the worktable in front of him
is from a dentist's office.

Terrace Off Second Floor

The rocket in the foreground
is Leo's creation: it is twelve feet
high and was assembled mostly
from aluminum pails, buckets,
and garbage cans. On the other
side of the woodpile (there's a
woodstove in the living room),
is a Leo palm tree — its base is
a pedestal from a dentist's office,
its leaves are license plates.
The terrace is used for gardening
and for dining alfresco in good
weather. The indoor dining room
is just on the other side of the
door. The old stone building
glimpsed in the background is
an Episcopal church.

Backyard   l e f t

Leo whistles to his collection
of junk-composed animal
sculptures. A duck sits on a
birdbath in the middle of a
garden. A horse, almost
life-size, stands near the door.
Other animals include a pig,
another duck, a few dogs, and
a miniature African elephant.
Through the arched back
door, the center hallway
that leads to the front door
can be glimpsed.

Lenore Tawney
Weaver

I didn't think about the sign I saw in the entry area until I had been there for quite a while. It said: "Be kind to delivery men." This seems to show Lenore's point of view on life. At the age of eighty-six, she lives in a world apart that she has created inside her New York City loft. People enter her space, and deliver their presence. She reminds herself to be thoughtful to them, to treat them kindly. Visitors have to take their shoes off when they come in. Lenore has ways of making you conscious of her surroundings.

The loft is eighty feet long and thirty feet wide, with twelve-foot-high ceilings. The windows, nine on each wall, look north and south, onto a New York City street and, at the other end, the backs of buildings. The whole place is painted white—the walls, the ceiling, even the floor—and almost everything in it is white. Diffused light shines through the muslin-covered windows and reflects off the floor. It is like being inside a big cloud: the whiteness and reflections give unity to the room.

It is clear that Lenore likes monochromatic schemes. Her collage pieces, her floor and shelf arrangements, her weavings and "cloud" hangings—all are monotonic, or mostly neutral. They rely on line and shape and texture to give them impact. The only intense colors are in Lenore's clothing and in the flowers around the room.

Her whole loft is one big working space, with segmented areas for storage, everyday living, and contemplation. Lenore uses her space to display groups of ideas together, or to explore an idea that she wants to keep looking at and thinking about; her working environment is always within reach. With her work so close at hand she can get up in the morning with an idea, and the materials are right there to realize it.

She lives in the city to be close to museums, supply sources, gallery people, and her friends. The work of her friends is displayed throughout the loft, and I found myself looking at their work in relation to Lenore because their pieces reflect her own style and personality—economical, spiritual, and perhaps a little obscure. She has different-sized pots, some of them closed up, by ceramist Toshiko Takaezu. She has one charcoal drawing, by her friend Joe Barnes, that is simply a horizontal line bisecting a piece of handmade paper. And she has a grid construction by an old friend and former neighbor, artist Agnes Martin. She also has collections, such as Southwest Native American pottery and Greek pottery, from different times in her life. Standing on a shelf that leans rather casually against the wall is a carved wooden angel, about two feet high, with its arms spread. She has had it for a very long time, and I have the feeling it is a presence she has become accustomed to.

Her furniture is mostly practical, worktables and chairs, Japanese chests with iron hardware that looks handmade, and three-legged stools that she bought directly from Wharton Esherick, a very well-known woodworker and innovator in the thirties and forties. Many of her possessions are things she just picked up, such as the Naugahyde chair she found in her building's elevator that she painted over, of course, white. Another reason she lives in the city is the availability of all the stuff on the street.

Entrance | On the other side of these glass shelves are the elevator and entrance to Lenore Tawney's New York City loft, so you have a peek into the place before you actually go inside. The shelves hold a varied collection of pots. The row of all-white pots was collected in Greece; there are also some replicas of ancient Greek figures, portions of a turtle shell, and the skull of a small alligator. The bottom shelf holds pots by ceramist Toshiko Takaezu; more of her pots sit on the floor. The chest with all the little drawers is one of Lenore's collage chests. The framed object on the top, at left, is a wooden hand that she found on a beach; near it is a kinetic, clocklike sculpture. The duck decoy atop the white pedestal is collaged with papers, an artistic device of which she is fond.

Arrangement Near East Wall

The tall, treelike structure is a ten-foot-tall African ladder, probably from Mali. Near it are wooden chests that might be Japanese, with iron drawer pulls. On top of them are four duck decoys; Lenore prefers the unpainted ones. The cloth-covered mannequin with wool knee socks and iron feet looks tiny in relation to the ladder; it is actually about forty inches tall. Above its neck, in lieu of a head, is a conch shell. The child's rocker was discovered in a New Jersey barn shop. The pot in the foreground is an early stoneware vessel by famed American ceramist Peter Voulkos. The arrangement to the right of the pot includes an artist's articulated wooden mannequin wearing a doll's straw hat; inside the box she sits on are a pair of child's moccasins and an ear of Indian corn; to the right of the box is a black and white rock Lenore found and liked. On the left hang two of Lenore's knotted "cloud" structures, which she has been making in recent years instead of traditional weavings. They are actually three-dimensional, and you could stand under them or in them. When exhibited, they are suspended from the ceiling with invisible monofilament wires and look as though they hang free in space. The white curtain behind them covers a storage area.

Loft, Facing Window Area on North

The walls in the eighty-foot-long loft are painted a shimmering white; the floor is white as well. Translucent white curtains at all the windows (nine on each side) soften the light. The tables in back are all work areas. Through the tangle of the work space, two of Lenore's radiating line drawings in black and red can be glimpsed on the floor. In the middle ground on the right, facing the work area, is a Naugahyde chair that Lenore found in the elevator of her building; she rescued it and painted it white. The dignified tall white columns lining the loft are structural concrete. The three-legged stools scattered around the open area were bought by Lenore directly from Wharton Esherick, the esteemed American woodworker. In the foreground is one of Lenore's spatial arrangements, consisting of natural and man-made objects that were found, bought, or donated.

Lenore scavenges on all levels. She looks at what service she can get out of what she finds—how she can use it in her work—rather than at its monetary value. It would not matter if something were made of gold if it worked in a piece. She especially likes things that other people have used up for themselves and that she can reuse. She uses a lot from the natural world in her work, almost always in connection with the earth colors and neutral tones of her weavings—porcupine quills, small animal or bird skulls, stones, sticks.

In the mid forties, Lenore was in Chicago studying with a group of famous, exiled European artists. She studied drawing with Laszlo Moholy-Nagy and sculpture with Alexander Archipenko. She also studied weaving; she spent a summer working intensely with the Finnish weaver Martta Taipale. By the early sixties she was exhibiting her own experimental weaving, which involved working with open warps, weaving off the loom, and hanging the weavings not against the wall but in space, like sculpture. Soon afterward she began to make collages and Joseph Cornell–like collage boxes. More recently she has been creating enormous three-dimensional hangings—her "clouds."

Lenore has a number of what she calls "collage chests" in her loft. Inside these chests are rows and rows of little drawers, into which she puts objects you can hold in your hand: small bowls, old tools, balls of smoothly wound twine, bird feathers, a nest with a tiny egg inside, rolled manuscripts and parchments, wooden sample foot molds, dolls' arms and hands, seashells. Creating the chests is like structuring a weaving—planning patterns and arrangements while always keeping in mind the appearance of the whole.

She also has a lot of jars and bottles, some empty, some filled. Her bed is behind glass, enclosed in a transparent space like a Portuguese man-of-war, in an envelope you can see through. The area serves no other purpose—it's just a place to go into to sleep, a space with one object in it, very deliberate. She used to have a chair hanging in the loft wrapped inside a kind of gauze bag, and that's what the bedroom made me think of—that chair, like a seed in a pod, or a yolk in the center of an egg. All the containers she has collected, and the drawers she puts things in, give a powerful impression of her consciousness of the container as a theme.

Northwest Corner of Loft   l e f t

Toshiko Takaezu's huge closed pot dominates this corner. The small form on the wooden block in front of it is the maquette for the piece. The articulated plastic figure covered with paper collage is a work in progress. What is missing is a full-size cello with its front removed, the open interior filled with hundreds of bits of paper, all copies of famous composers' manuscript scores. The cello used to be alongside the figure, clasped by the mannequin's left arm and hand; it has been temporarily mislaid. The figure was made about twenty years ago. A minimalist drawing by Lenore's friend Joe Barnes hangs on the wall to the right of the big pot. Items on the windowsill, the shelf beneath it, and the floor include a basket full of eggshells on a little stool; an ostrich egg; a bowl filled with glass eyes that Lenore got from her friend Ferne Jacobs, a well-known basket artist; and an old doll with a cloth body.

Loft, Detail

Everything in this picture has been collaged with printed and music manuscript paper, except the legs of the stool. Not even the wooden shoe form under the stool has escaped Lenore's paste pot.

Loft, Detail

Crow Woman has the body of an old doll and the head of a long-dead bird, maybe a crow. A wooden stick to which a fishing fly is attached has been substituted for one arm. The "aquarium" has been splashed with blue paint to simulate water; the fish is a found piece of driftwood.

Loft, Detail

This is one of Lenore's assemblage chests with most of the drawers open, revealing its curious contents, including dolls' arms, little glass jars containing something mysterious, a wooden pear, a cloven hoof, a wooden alphabet block, some small bowls, and some rolled scrolls.

Portrait

Lenore, in a red dress she made herself, poses with her orange and white cat, Angel. On the wall behind her and to the left is a black cloth that is photocopier-printed with Lenore's hands and Rudolf Nureyev's feet. The black linen square under it is entitled *Small Dark Cloud on the Horizon*. Another collage chest sits on top of a key-slot cabinet and is filled with a personal miscellany that includes string, wooden balls and etchings of balls, dried daffodils, sand dollars, small porcelain cups, birds' nests, and skulls.

In fact, she uses the loft itself as one big container or collage chest, arranging objects in various places and patterns throughout the large, white space. The painted floor is a white ocean, the arrangements are islands you float between. Some of these islands are developing; some are totally developed. Some are worlds in infancy; some house functional tools or waiting materials. Some read as a mature world—all finished. On one table might be objects she just picked up off the street and has not yet used in any way. And another table may hold tools she is using at that moment.

So Lenore's working space is her entire surroundings. Each arrangement in her loft is open to interpretation —in progress or complete, depending on your point of view. The gear patterns and stones that have been placed near a column, the African ladder against a wall, the mannequins, the beam rescued from a burned-out building, the muslin "spirit bags," the muslin bag that looks like a fish—perhaps they will all stay as they are for a while, or maybe Lenore will move them tomorrow. It does not matter—the effect of the constant transition is natural and somehow soothing.

I think Lenore develops her visions on both a conscious and subconscious level. Everything she creates is uniquely her own because it comes from her center. She has an innate respect for the natural environment, for the earth. All of the things she has picked up on streets, beaches, and wherever else she finds objects, make up the threads of her work. There is an interweaving for Lenore of her work, her life, her living space, and her beliefs. It is what gives a great deal of the quality to her work.

Diane Kempler

Ceramist

Diane and Bernhard Kempler's home, on a tree-lined street in Atlanta, Georgia, is much like the other houses on the block, except for the handsome front door with its arched glass. But the moment the front door is opened, the surprises start.

Diane and Bernhard came to Atlanta from the Northeast when Bernhard accepted a post teaching psychology at Georgia State University. They thought they would stay for a few years — that was almost thirty years ago. They bought this house in 1971. Meanwhile, their children grew up in it, Diane went through many shifts in her career, and the house survived three renovations.

It was the most-recent renovation, in the late eighties, that resulted in the high drama of the center of the house. And if the center of the house is its heart, then the foyer that leads to it is the major artery. Opening the front door you are instantly standing not in a hallway, but in an art gallery.

It seems appropriate that a visitor, who will have climbed the forty-two steps that lead to the front door, is greeted with a blast of light and an eclectic collection of art. It is a foreshadowing of the house itself, which ranges from cozy Victorian to an Arts and Crafts style to ultramodern. The white walls in the foyer are bathed in light that pours through a row of skylights and illuminates the art, which includes a wooden figure from Indonesia, an aboriginal Australian painting, some pieces by Diane, some graphic art, and an old settle on which to rest and look.

The door at the end of the gallery opens onto an even more unusual space — the central kitchen area. Kitchens can be handsome or workaday, cramped or roomy, cheerful or dark, but rarely are they rooms that stop you in your tracks. This kitchen looks like a stage on which, at a given signal, a drama may unfold. It is built on a platform and all around it is space — and a remarkable stairway. The kitchen space also has a skylight, and everything is gleaming and white, with the same sort of long, unbroken lines as the long foyer. Because Diane and Bernhard were determined not to let anything disturb the outer curve of the cabinets and counter along the wall, they decided against having a standard refrigerator. Instead, they installed two small refrigerators under the counter.

"We didn't want the kitchen to be a separate room," Diane explains. "We wanted a sense of openness that would be part of the living space. But we had it put on a platform so that in stepping up or down it gets differentiated from the rest of the house — a separate entity within the whole. I think instead of looking like a kitchen, it is like another piece of furniture."

The high-ceilinged open space with its polished oak floors was once a solid block of rooms — the old kitchen, three bedrooms, and two baths. Now it is the core area for the Kemplers' annual New Year's Day bash. In fact it is the setting for numerous parties, which vary considerably in size and frequency, from a potluck supper of Diane's with friends to a faculty meeting with Bernhard's colleagues to a sit-down dinner for eighteen in the formal dining room. In all these cases the crowd starts out gathered around the curving marble worktable at the edge of the kitchen platform, chatting and getting their drinks.

If the stairway opposite the kitchen appears to float, maybe it is more from a sense of water than of ambient air, and that is just what the Kemplers wanted. They

Sitting Room | The light-filled sitting room on the other side of the kitchen overlooks the garden. The sofa table was put together from an old wrought-iron base that probably once held a sewing machine, and a marble top from what Diane calls the "marble death yard" — a surplus-and-discard place for odd pieces of marble. The figure at the far left is a Northwest Native American puppet; Diane's brother obtained it from the British Columbian artist John Livingston for Diane's birthday. The bookcase contains a number of collected objects, including three African bronze fish on the top shelf, a piece from 1979 by Diane below it, and Javanese rod puppets in the opening to the right of Diane's piece. The rug was found in a market in Jaffa, Israel.

explained to Atlanta sculptor Scott Gilliam that they wanted "the image of running water." The seemingly suspended stair ascends on wooden treads attached to a steel spine and a curtain of steel mesh; it gives you the feeling of a waterfall or a stream wandering over flat rocks. "And the stairs move a little when you walk on them," adds Diane, so that they directly convey a gentle sensation of water in motion.

Diane does not think of the house as particularly large, but it does accommodate a variety of activities and contrasts in visual moods. And it has one particular charm of older houses (it was built in 1914)—little rooms and nooks that add to the interest of the space and, consequently, to living in it. At the front of the house, parallel to the foyer, are the living and dining rooms. The living room (not shown) is the most conventional. The love seats are grouped at right angles around the fireplace, and there are some overstuffed chairs in a little alcove and a Persian rug on the floor. In another alcove off the living room is the piano. Diane feels it's a warm, comfortable room that "entertains well."

A large opening flanked by elegant old columns and built-in cabinets leads into the expansive dining room, centered with a very large table that can comfortably seat eighteen to twenty people. The different sets of dining room chairs were found in secondhand stores: a Gothic Revival style and a somewhat more modern style with turned legs and half-upholstered backs. What unifies this diverse suite of dining room furniture is that Diane painted all of it white. The furniture is not only eye-catching, it is reminiscent of the British Arts and Crafts movement as well as of turn-of-the-century Vienna Secession design.

Off in the other direction, at the back of the house, is a little breakfast area. There's also a sitting room, on the other side of the kitchen, that overlooks the garden through an expanse of windows. The sitting room has a ceiling-to-floor bookcase and matched, old-fashioned Victorian seating—a sofa and two easy chairs covered in a floral fabric. The garden was renovated only a few years ago. The Kemplers hired a "landscape person" to choose the plantings, and a "pond person" to put in the goldfish pond, but they did most of the work themselves. Diane wanted something that combined the economical aesthetic of a Japanese garden with the fresh informality of an English garden. Like the steel staircase in the interior space, the path through the garden has a sense of flow rather like water. Framed with shrubs, flower beds, and trees, flat stones form the stairs that lead up to stone terraces; the path climbs gently as it progresses away from the house.

Dining Room

The table and the two different sets of chairs were all found in antique shops. The table, which is set with an antique lace cloth for formal dinners, is impressive and elegant. Japanese prints on the far wall above the wainscoting were replaced recently with wall sconces, and track lighting in the ceiling has given way to recessed light for a more ambient effect. The window on the far wall is actually an adjoining alcove furnished with two Victorian chairs, an antique hutch, and a twig table. On the far left is one of the columns that flank the entrance to the living room.

Detail

When Diane returned to ceramics after an eight-year hiatus, this was the first piece she made. An arrangement of a dozen grouped figures, nine of which are shown here, the piece celebrates both her return to ceramics and the renovation of the house. Called *Celebration of the House*, it includes figures with little house shapes for heads or bodies. The four porcelain platters in the background, at the top of the paneled wainscoting, represent Diane's early work.

Foyer Gallery

The front door, which was moved from the back when the house was renovated a few years ago, was one of the features that sold the Kemplers on the house. This hallway was added on and serves as both an entryway and a gallery for displaying some of the couple's collection and some work of Diane's. In the foreground, back toward the door, can be seen an Indonesian wooden house post, an Australian aboriginal painting, three curved and painted wooden bowls from the Asmat tribe of southern Indonesia, a wall piece Diane made that is suggestive of an altar, an Inuit print from the Canadian Arctic, and a gouache painting by Janie Geiser. The wooden settle, opposite, is old. On the floor opposite the settle is a little white porcelain chair that Diane made years ago.

Detail

The wall with built-in niches is opposite the Indonesian house post in the foyer. There are small African figures in the top niche, a Guatemalan mask, a work of Diane's, a Zuni feather fetish, a bust by Kerri Wooten (another Atlanta ceramist), and another African figure.

Like many craftsmen and their families, the Kemplers have collected art and artifacts from all over the world, as well as the work of people they know. The decor of their home changes from room to room. Diane explains that she and Bernhard have broad-ranging tastes and see no reason to restrict themselves to "one definite aesthetic"—nor do they feel compelled "to make things match." This gives them freedom. As Diane says, "It allows us to live with whatever we want to live with."

The human form is often depicted in the work they collect. This is not surprising when you see that Diane's work, especially for the last few years, has centered on the human form and its connection to nature. Diane first encountered ceramics when she was working at a crafts center in Massachusetts after college—she is from New York originally—and found that it was what she wanted to do with her life. About twelve years ago, after working successfully in the field, she began to wonder whether ceramics was, as she says, "fulfilling any of my needs." So she stopped for eight years and took a job as director of a puppetry-arts-center museum, and continued to teach and work as a freelance installation and graphics designer. At the end of that period she realized that she needed her own work back again, and she returned to it with changed vision and recharged energy.

Her work now—all sculptural—focuses on the abstracted human torso. The pieces are large, but economical in both line and tone. She expresses connections with nature with the symbolic use of tree forms, root shapes, or other green growth. The ideas of regeneration and change have had a central role in her work for a long time, and those concerns have inevitably spilled over into her house, which over the years has changed its inner forms and opened itself to space and light.

Kempler's Work

This grouping of Diane's recent ceramic sculptures in her studio demonstrates her interest in combining the human figure with leaf, frond, thorn, and branch images, as well as roots (represented by the legs). These earthenware "root maidens" are both glazed and unglazed and are constructed in sections. The work in the foreground is over five feet tall.

Steel Staircase

On the other side of the foyer door is a large open space defined by the unusual staircase and the kitchen, opposite. The staircase is made of maple treads and a curtain of steel-mesh risers affixed to a steel spine. The railings comprise steel piping and cables. The stairs lead up to the master bedroom and bath and Diane's study. A sculpture by Diane stands under the balcony between two photographs by Michael Kenna, an English photographer, and a graphic work in conte crayon by Atlanta artist Katherine Mitchell. On the wall at the foot of the stairs is a wooden piece from New Guinea known as a "spirit hook."

Kitchen

The entire kitchen is set on a platform in the open area at the center of the house. The worktable is white marble; the counters are wood, lacquered white. The sink is next to the worktable. As in every other room in the house, the kitchen is a display area for the Kemplers' collections. On top of the counters, a painted wood mermaid from Mexico shares space under the high ceiling with three ceramic figures by Diane and a pair of salt-glazed covered pots by ceramist Robert Turner. The oak-floored open area serves as a gathering place when the couple entertains. A hanging made by Diane occupies the wall just inside the foyer door, opposite the staircase (see detail).

Hanging in Open Area

Small ceramic figures by Diane hang within a wire net suspended from nylon, making interesting shadows, in this 1980 piece called *Ark*. It hangs in the open area just beyond the foyer door.

Portrait | Diane in her garden with sculpture.

Garden
left | This area used to be a more anonymous arrangement of grass and trees. The Kemplers wanted something with more grace, charm, and art, but also "a garden that looks as if it had been here forever." The natural branch stair railings lead to the first of two stone terraces. In the far background is one of Diane's sculptures, with a sculpture by Ron Myers in the foreground. The garden is about seventy-five feet long but seems even larger, perhaps because of the flow of the stone stairs and the multiple levels that carry the eye.

Sam Maloof
Woodworker

The home of Sam and Alfreda Maloof is like a living organism: it keeps growing and changing, full of the work, interest, and memories of a lifetime.

Set in a six-acre lemon grove, it is surrounded by the lush density of nature. Coming through the courtyard you have to duck to keep the nuts from a mature walnut tree from hitting you on the head. The house and its setting are idyllic. They are also an island.

When the Maloofs moved to this southern California farming area forty years ago, the population of the village was one thousand and its inhabitants met each other daily at the post office. Now the town is part of an urban/suburban sprawl — complete with housing developments, highways, and shopping malls — while Sam and his family remain enveloped in older American dreams.

Born in southern California to Lebanese-immigrant parents, Sam was the seventh of nine children in a large, close-knit family. He seemed to have been born with an interest in working with wood. As a child he was always carving, everything from little wooden trucks to a baking paddle (which his sisters used for many decades). He also loved to draw, and for a few years his drawing had the upper hand. After he graduated from high school he worked in graphic arts until 1941, when he joined the Army. Although he went back to graphics at the end of World War II, he found that working in two dimensions did not satisfy him anymore. By then he was working for, and had become friendly with, a number of potential mentors in the visual arts — a painter, a sculptor, an architect, and an industrial designer. He drew knowledge from this broad array of artists and listened hard to them, pairing what he heard with his own native instincts.

Sam met Alfreda in 1947. She had been an art teacher and a crafts cooperative organizer at pueblos and reservations in the Southwest. She was attending art school, on leave from her work on the reservations, when they met and married. Freda fixed up their little apartment as well as she could, but Sam felt they needed new furniture. When a contractor he knew gave him some specially treated plywood, he made his first set of furnishings, for their home. Later, a magazine ran an illustrated article on their home, and that was the turning point: Sam decided to strike out on his own as a woodworker. Word spread quickly and the commissions began to grow. One early commission was from the well-known industrial designer Henry Dreyfuss. Sam was becoming established.

He dreamed of living in the country, but they did not have much money to buy a house. But in 1953 he and Freda managed to find a "livable" shack, with one nice avocado tree, on two acres of land, and they bought the rest of the property on "time." His workshop was a dirt-floor chicken coop with a ceiling so low that he had to bend to avoid bumping his head. As soon as he was able to, he built a real workshop, and eventually he replaced the shack with the first unit of his house.

What he built turned out to be not a finished house but the nucleus of a constantly expanding home. That first section of his now sprawling domain contained one large room that functioned as bedroom, kitchen, and dining room, and a small bath and bedrooms for his two young children.

The growth of the house has been a pragmatic process. Whenever Sam accumulated enough two-by-fours, he would build another wing. With his developed instincts, he built the house as he builds his furniture: to look good and to work well. He put up additions without the aid of drawings, and calculated alignments with only his practiced eye. In his book he wrote that if anything turned out to be a bit off, it would "give the house a little character." In fact, many parts of the house started as one thing and then evolved into another.

Front Door Entryway | Rows of wood and cement columns lead up to the front door.

A bedroom became a sitting room with a sleeping loft, creating a walk-through to another bedroom. The carport turned into Freda's office.

The house is U-shaped. The first section built was the center, where the public spaces are—the sitting, dining, and food preparation area. Down one side of the house runs a string of bedrooms, starting with the master bedroom. Down the other side run the workshops and lumber storage buildings. To a woodworker, these storage buildings seem like a treasure trove—all the things you might make with all that beautiful wood!

Sam can walk right from his shop into the kitchen. In the kitchen there are multiple stoves and sinks, about five altogether, as well as many places to sit down and eat. This is the best way to meet the needs of all the comings and goings in the house—the Maloofs must have a few thousand visitors each year. They are wonderful hosts and it is surprising that Sam finds enough time to work.

It is a rambling house, with plenty of room to sit and rest or read a book or talk. Tranquil, quiet, somewhat dark, and full of wandering space, it is like a labyrinth, full of chambers and corners and balconies. The bones of the house are fairly visible—exposed post-and-beam construction and curving lintels between rooms. Most of the doors have unique latches Sam made so that you can see exactly how they work. And, of course, there is a lot of woodwork in the house.

While some craftsmen prefer to have their studios separate from their homes, having everything together is essential to Sam. He likes having his family nearby too: their son, Slimen, has his own workshop and residence across the lemon grove, and their daughter, Marilou, lives in the neighborhood, so the workshop is often full of grandchildren trying to be helpful. This interaction of home and work is simply Sam's way of life. He says he is often asked how he manages not to succumb to the desire to lie down or read a book, when the means for relaxation are so close at hand. It is a matter of discipline, he responds. When he needs a stretch or a change of pace, he steps outside and does a little planting or watering (although Freda is the head gardener).

Sam calls his home "the house that grew." I think it grew in a lot of ways, not just physically. To judge by old pictures of the interior, the house was formerly very clean and spare, with red, black, and yellow decor and burlap on the walls. Even as recently as a decade ago it had a certain spareness. Now the colors have been toned down and blend more richly; there is more pattern, detail, and complexity, greater depth and softness.

Portrait | The Maloofs outside their home.

Kitchen

Seen from the front door entrance, the usually busy kitchen seems quiet and well organized. Behind the counter on the left are two stoves, side-by-side: there are often a number of mouths to feed, from family to friends, assistants, and distant travelers. The kitchen has three sinks. Over the center cabinet are family photos; above them is a shelf with wooden toys that Sam bought out of the back of the toy maker's station wagon. One of the casseroles on the middle counter is by well-known ceramist Karen Karnes.

Door, Detail

The door that leads out from the kitchen to the deck and the lemon grove has a handsome latch made by Sam, who made several of the latches in the house.

His work is very much concerned with furniture as furniture, and not just as a means of self-expression. He wants his pieces to sit well, be comfortable, and show good use of the wood. He is very respectful of the woodworking traditions of the past, and people like and respect his affinity for wood.

Sam's early furniture was influenced by Scandinavian design, which was popular in the fifties, when he was establishing himself in the field. Today his style is very much his own. He is known and respected for all his work, but it is his chairs, settees, and rockers that are his signature pieces; a number of them are in American museums, as well as in the White House and the Vice President's mansion. Sam is one of the few craftsmen who have attained widespread popular appeal. His success has resulted in awards and public recognition, for which he is very grateful. With the aim of "giving back" to the community, he does public service work in his field, gives workshops and lectures, and passes on his expertise to apprentices in his shop.

Perhaps his famous chairs and rockers are his most striking works because they are most akin to the active, welcoming side of his personality. He writes in his book, "I do not try consciously to make my pieces reflect their maker, but I hope that my furniture is an outgoing part of my personality and my way of think-ing. I hope that it is vibrant, alive, and friendly to the people who use it. . . . I want my chairs to invite a person to sit . . . to embrace that person, give comfort."

The core of Sam's attitude toward his work and his life is spiritual, and his own outlook is full of thankful-ness and quiet joy.

Dining Area   *left*

Sam's black walnut dining table with wooden-hinged leaves is in the foreground. The seating consists of three-place settees upholstered in black leather, on either side of the table. Sam's hutch has a drop front that could double as a writing table. The grand doorway has leaded-glass lights that were salvaged from a house owned by one of Sam's nieces. The red brick floor, in Santa Fe style, is enlivened by a Chinese rug. The chandeliers above the table, in wood and wrought iron, were made by a friend, Carl Jennings. The living room's Scandinavian iron stove can be glimpsed through the doorway.

Family Room   *above*

The posts holding up the handsome arched lintel are of eucalyptus; the wedges under the lintel in the corners are there to pick up the slack when the wood dries out. Sam both engineered and built the arrangement. Two of Sam's most famous pieces can be seen in this room — the rocker, foreground, and the double settee — editions of which are in two different American museums. The upholstered armchair in the corner was one of Sam's earlier creations (1949). He traded it for a fifty-dollar radio, but later reobtained it — for appreciably more. The handsome red oriental rug on the brick floor, and the various rugs and textiles hanging over the railing of the balcony, add warmth, color, and pattern to the room. The window in the background looks out over the lemon grove.

**Balcony Above
Living Room Area**

The Zuni, Acoma,
and Zia pottery
of the Southwest
has been collected
over the years
by Sam and Freda;
above the pots
is a painting by
a long-time friend
and mentor of Sam's,
artist Millard Sheets.

Tower Area

A dining table and chairs in walnut, of
Sam's design, sit under the "tower room"
fiery turn-of-the-century carousel horses,
stripped to the natural wood, are bathed
in the light coming in from above. The
handsome hanging lamps over the table
are actually industrial lighting. California
wood turner Bob Stockdale made the
turned bowls on the dining table.

Sitting Room

This small room off the balcony area
is also known as the "tree house room."
It is flooded with light from the triangular
clerestory windows. The beam seen just
below the windows, across the top of the
room, is the trunk of a eucalyptus tree.
Among the objects on the surface at the
right are Japanese tea ceremony containers
and basket sculpture by well-known
California basket maker Kay Sekimachi.
(The painting diagonally above them
is by Sam and Freda's daughter-in-law,
Kathryn Maloof.) The prints on the wall
in the alcove are Japanese. The rocker
in the center is Sam's.

Guest Room Area

The guest room sitting area has a bed under the balcony, as well as a sleeping loft. The beautiful spiral staircase Sam made leads up to the loft. The room combines Southwest Native American and contemporary American pottery collections. Indian blankets draped over the sleeping balcony railing add vivid color to the otherwise neutral-toned room. Up a few steps, the glassed-in atrium leads to another guest room.

Bedroom, Detail

Baskets on the floor behind the rocker on the right hold Navaho and Appalachian dolls Freda collected, as well as Native American moccasins that Freda wore when she worked with Native Americans on a pueblo near Santa Fe.

Master Bedroom right

Everyone is surprised when they see this headboardless bed in the master bedroom. For sitting up and reading there is a daybed (not seen) on the other side of the screen. An iron stove is in the background. The pup stretched out on the bed is ceramic. Two of Sam's rockers, in bird's-eye maple and figured maple, flank the Franklin stove. The model train set on the structure over the stove was Sam's birthday gift to his one-year-old son in 1950. Most of the objects in the room, as well as the textiles, are Southwest Native American. The watercolor portrait of the Indian woman is by Winold Reiss, a friend of Freda's.

Richard Mafong
Jon Eric Riis Metalsmith
Weaver

The word *hospitality* is automatically paired with the word *Southern* in many minds, and in a house that hospitality often begins in the entry hall. It is hard not to feel welcome when you are shown into a foyer of such open and generous size that it is really a room.

Richard Mafong and Jon Riis have such a hall in their house, on a tree-lined street in a section of Atlanta that has seen bad days but is on the rise. The turn-of-the-century house they bought in 1982 was originally the comfortable home of a well-off family, and then a fraternity house, and then a boarding house that became badly run down.

It took Richard and Jon three years of hands-on labor to make it respectable, and they are still fine-tuning the restoration. The interior was stripped down to the laths, but they retained the original layout as well as the multiple fireplaces (a couple of beauties were found in the dining room and sitting room under layers of ugly paint).

The house, its walk framed in ivy, is a symmetrical Georgian Revival brick with a wraparound porch and a slate roof. But the symmetry stops at the front door. Inside, the visitor first encounters the grand hall, which holds a baby grand piano that you could almost overlook — probably the ultimate test for spaciousness. Beyond the columned hall on one side are the dining room and kitchen area (the kitchen and the bathrooms are the only modern parts of the house). On the other side are double parlors — a luxury of genteel living that went out with the twentieth century.

Richard and Jon share a reputation among friends, acquaintances, and colleagues for the warmth and charm of their home and their graciousness as hosts. They also share their lives. They have been friends and companions since the early seventies, when both were teaching at Georgia State University, where Richard remains an associate professor of art. Their house reflects their backgrounds and experiences. Jon, a tapestry weaver and designer, is accustomed to achieving complex effects with pattern, texture, and color (he left full-time teaching in 1976 to establish his own business). Richard, a craftsman who works in precious metals who has made work ranging from architectural panels to sterling silver tea services to jewelry in gold, silver, and gemstones, obviously enjoys the sheen and opulence of beautiful surfaces. In addition to Richard's metalsmithing, and Jon's work with corporate and public tapestry commissions, the two have traveled many times to the Far East for designing and consulting assignments, as well as to Guatemala and the Caribbean. Richard has a tie to the rich culture of China through his parents, as well as to Hispanic culture, with its high colors and elaborate decorations, from his childhood in Mexico.

Entrance Hall | The large entry hall sets the tone for the rest of the spacious, sumptuous turn-of-the-century house, furnished with Chinese antiques and fascinating collections. The walls are painted a soft gray-green, the moldings, a creamy white. The original columns are painted in a faux marble finish, matching the two marble fireplaces that were uncovered in the dining room and sitting room during renovations. Chinese rugs warm the heart-of-pine wood floor. To the left (not seen) is the hall's sitting area, complete with baby grand piano, comfortable chairs, and a black marble fireplace. In the right foreground, standing on a Victorian pedestal, is one of their extensive collections of nineteenth-century Guatemalan and Mexican santos; this one is San Rafael. In front of the wall between the doors, beneath a Japanese print, is an elaborate black and gold lacquered Chinese clothes rack in which hangs Jon's tapestry *The Diver*. The door at left leads into the formal dining room; the opening at right leads into the hallway that goes to the large modern kitchen at the back of the house, and an outdoor deck. Halfway down this hallway are the stairs to the lower level workshops — Jon's large weaving studio and Richard's smaller metal shop. The studios are on ground level at the back of the house.

Hallway

The hallway leading to the back stairs and kitchen area is another venue for displaying Jon and Richard's handsome collections; they have shown a considerable talent not just for finding, but for displaying their treasures. The niche in the wall holds a series of Richard's small silver containers. Behind them is a painted Oriental scroll. The Chinese altar table beneath the niche is covered with a chrysanthemum-embroidered Japanese obi, on which sit various glass vessels, from a contemporary American piece to a Tiffany glass vase and a French turn-of-the century piece. On the wall at the back is a large nineteenth-century Native American painting on fabric. Beneath it, on the floor, are French pickling and oil jars from Haiti.

There is a concern throughout their house not just with the objects and furniture as such, but with the interplay of color, texture, form, and light. Richard and Jon seem to have a fine sense of how to play off all these qualities against one another, and to balance them successfully. They have collected nineteenth-century santos from Guatemala and Mexico, fabric paintings from India, objects from Southeast Asia, and many things from China, ranging from ceremonial tables to children's hats and a house full of antique Chinese furniture. Although their house is filled to its eleven-foot ceilings with all kinds of objects, textiles, and antique and modern furniture, everything is so well arranged that the effect is one of order and tranquillity. In the daytime, the blinds are often drawn against the light, producing a calming dimness that seems to isolate the rooms in place and time. At night the light is warm and glowing, and brings the rooms and their rich furnishings to life.

The dining room is quiet and dignified, full of gleaming wood surfaces—a Chinese antique dining table surrounded by high-backed chairs, the sideboard and mantel lined with objects. The front parlor is all creamy tones and light colors, while the adjoining sitting room is darker, more masculine, with a mix of furnishings from leather-and-chrome modern to Asian artifacts.

Upstairs, the ambiance of comfort and elegance is continued in the three bedrooms and a wonderful library that has walls of books—mostly art books—and deep couches to sit on and lose yourself in a world of scholarship.

Richard and Jon have applied many of their personal qualities and interests to their home—their love of beauty, their scholarly knowledge, their aesthetic perceptiveness, their feeling for and experience with fine craftsmanship, their design acumen, their business sense, the fruits of their travels and international connections, and their heritage, both acquired and direct.

To have your home say so much about you and do so much for you, and for it to be a place of beauty and serenity enjoyed by others as well, is a remarkable achievement. Richard and Jon's is an elegant, fascinating house; it is that old cliché refreshed—a feast for the eyes and a treat for the mind.

Portrait | Richard and Jon on the porch of their home.

133

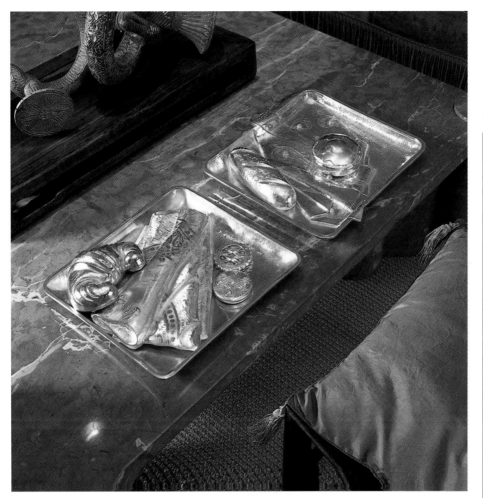

Parlor Detail

Front Parlor

The front parlor is light-toned, almost pastel in contrast with the adjoining back parlor. It features a Victorian white marble fireplace. The 1850 mantel is flanked by a pair of sofas upholstered in a pale green fabric, patterned with almost invisible flowers alternating with a cream and gold stripe. The pillows on the sofa are covered in old Japanese obi cloth. An eighteenth-century gilded English mirror hangs above the mantel, on which rest Swedish candlesticks that belonged to Jon's great-grandmother. The blue and white vase on the mantel is Ming. The walls are covered in silk that was hand painted in Sung-dynasty style by two Atlanta residents, Lailani and Anho Nan. On a Chinese stand to the left of the fireplace is a pot from the Han dynasty; to the right, in a standing frame, is a small Japanese screen. The marble coffee table is by contemporary Italian architect and designer Gae Aulenti; it holds, among other things, wooden head ornaments from Sumatra and a pair of vermeil confections whipped up by Richard (see detail).

In an eclectic mix in the hallway, nineteenth-century santos from Guatemala are arrayed across a twentieth-century Chinese altar table.

Sitting Room (Back Parlor)

The sitting room is actually the back half of an old-fashioned double parlor. With its dark, rich tones, it would be an inviting place to relax on winter nights. Modern black leather and chrome armchairs designed by Mies Van Der Rohe face each other across a contemporary wooden cube coffee table made of a light burl wood. Jon and Richard's chow dog, looking like a cross between a lion and an old Chinese scholar, poses on the floor; he is called Xiong Xiong, which means "Brave Bear." The settle on the third side of the cube is a free adaptation of the turn-of-the-century British Arts and Crafts style. The Chinese Art Deco rug (1920) was found in Los Angeles. Among the small figures and brass candlesticks on the molded wood mantel, with its dark green marble surround, are two Burmese palace pieces. Against the windows, atop a large Burmese musical instrument case, is a leaping chimera. The walls are covered in another pattern of William Morris wallpaper. The coffee table holds Japanese boxes. Other art and artifacts around the room include items as diverse as a bowl by well-known American wood turner Ed Moulthrop, a twentieth-century African hat from Cameroon, Native American baskets, a small chrome table by Irish-French Art Deco designer Eileen Grey, and a bronze figure of Krishna.

Dining Room

The dining table is Chinese; the chairs around it are modern adaptations of designs by the Scottish Art Nouveau architect and designer Charles Rennie Mackintosh (as is other seating in the house). The three-section centerpiece on the table in silver, vermeil, and marble was made by Richard. The printed fabric on the chairs is from Jack Lenor Larsen. Against the back wall, an eighteenth-century Chinese altar table sits in front of the restored wainscoting and holds a variety of artifacts and art, including items as varied as a figure of Kuan-Yin, a piece of a New Guinean canoe prow, and vases holding cacti.

Detail

Beneath the William Morris wallpaper is Jon's tapestry depicting a hare, woven with metallic threads and freshwater pearls. It hangs on a nineteenth-century Chinese clothes rack, simpler than the one in the hallway. Above it hangs a framed fragment of a seventeenth-century chair panel woven in silk with gold threads. Beneath the tapestry are Burmese lacquered food containers.

Richard's Bedroom   l e f t

The large six-poster Chinese bed is teak. The wardrobe against the back wall is elm wood, and is also Chinese. With only a few exceptions—like the obviously contemporary desk lamp—all the furniture and objects are Chinese, including the rug and the orange patterned fabric draped over the desk chair.

Jon's Bedroom   f a r   l e f t

The richness and complexity of color and pattern in Jon's bedroom could only have been assembled by someone accustomed to dealing with these aesthetic components. The bed, described as Anglo-Chinese, was probably made for export: furniture that mixed Western and Chinese design elements was popular in Europe in the nineteenth century. The small red rug in front of the bed, as well as the bed hangings in a curious necktie shape, are Chinese; hanging on the wall behind the bed is a painted Burmese cotton temple hanging. Above the white marble Victorian fireplace is painted cotton from India, while on the mantel top are a variety of figures collected from West Bengal, Japan, and Germany. Drawn up to the Chinese table in the center of the room is a painted and beaded chair from India with an Indian pillow on the seat. The blue and white object in the center of the table is not ceramic, as one might suppose, but rather a stuffed fabric known as an elbow pillow; it too is Chinese.

Tom Joyce
Blacksmith

It is interesting how early many craftsmen show a talent for their vocation and then stay with it for the rest of their lives. Perhaps any calling is like that. Tom Joyce knew that he wanted to work with iron when he was sixteen. Living in a small town in New Mexico, as a young teenager he worked summers in a printing shop where there was also a small forge. Peter Wells, the owner and letterpress operator, was restoring old press parts for a museum in Santa Fe. At the end of each day, when the printing was done, they would turn to the primitive forge. Something about the contact with fire, about learning the mysteries of so ancient a trade, caught Tom's imagination. When Wells moved to Albuquerque a few years later, Tom took over the forge and the tools. When he dropped out of high school in his senior year, he supported himself by repairing farm implements and making pokers. He calls these years his alternative education, and judging by the results, his self-teaching was an extraordinary success.

Using the "self-education" method that Albert Paley was to turn to a few years later, Tom read extensively on his subject and visited museums for ideas and inspiration. He replicated old pieces, trying to draw out the secret of the artists' techniques. It should be remembered that when Tom and Albert decided in the early to mid seventies that they wanted to learn about hot-forging, blacksmithing was considered a quaint and dying art.

Tom is a resourceful, thoughtful, articulate man whom many consider to be one of the best architectural ironworkers in the country today. Over the course of his career he has lectured widely and been invited to participate in special projects and conferences abroad.

Tom's father was an archaeologist, who sometimes took him on excavations, and his mother was a quilter. As a child, Tom must have observed in his mother's work lovely patterns made from combinations of unexpected pieces; he must have seen, on his father's digs, how patience, skill, and perception can lead one to discover the secrets of the past. And finally, on his own at such an early age, he must have learned to be exploratory, inventive, and resourceful.

He has brought much of these observations and experiences, this reflectiveness and self-sufficiency, to his home in the hills of Santa Fe. With input from his wife, Julie, and a wish list from their two young daughters, Kate and Irene, Tom designed their house himself and served as his own contractor. The cabinetry was built to Tom's specifications, while Julie did the painting and staining throughout the house.

Although the dwelling is adobe, it was not built in the flat-roofed Santa Fe adobe style. Tom was impressed by the early Spanish colonial buildings he saw north of Santa Fe, and they influenced his design. The house has small windows, porches and balconies, a number of dormers, and a very deep roof overhang that is not only aesthetically pleasing, but also shades the house from the sun in the summer and protects the adobe.

The house was designed economically, to take advantage of natural forces while causing as little damage as possible to the surrounding land. The earth dug up during the excavation was saved, sifted, and used in the garden as topsoil and on the exterior walls (a mixture of mud, sand, and straw) and interior walls (mud plaster in the master bedroom). The metal roof is designed so that rainwater quickly slides down into gutters that drain, ultimately, into underground cisterns. The sun, through passive solar energy, is used as a

Portrait Tom's forge is in a large barnlike building on the grounds. Inside the large space are two coal hearths, one gas hearth, varying numbers of employees (depending on commissions), and three thousand tools, some of which date back to the twenties. Tom's anvil was brought back from a trip to England. The "iron" that modern blacksmiths work with is actually an iron alloy called mild steel.

source of heat as well as for food production. Tom's forge is also on the grounds, which cover five acres, complete with chickens, turkeys, and a large vegetable garden.

Tom established his own architectural blacksmithing company in Santa Fe at the age of twenty-two. His graceful ironwork is full of gentle curves and is hammered into varied designs for many purposes. He has forged everything from unique hardware for his own house to huge entry gates and railings, and his commissions have come from both private and public sources. Tom has a number of tools he found from the twenties, and he made a third of the three thousand tools he owns, most for specific jobs.

Julie is a dancer who heads an unusual dance company in Albuquerque. Called the Buen Viaje Dancers (meaning "good journey"), the troupe is composed of talented, creative people with various disabilities, aged twenty-five to forty-six, and performs all over the country. Julie is passionate about her work with the company. For a busy and transitioning family, their house has a cool, refreshing serenity and comfortable, uncluttered spaces that must seem like heaven to come home to.

There are no unnecessary rooms in this house. The two girls have their own bedroom and sitting room on the first floor. The master bedroom is on the second floor, with its own bath and a balcony that looks out over beautiful Santa Fe. For a house that is not large it offers a good deal of privacy. There is a guest bedroom upstairs, reachable by its own stairway—a little suite all by itself. Along the back of the house, connected to the kitchen, is the greenhouse that provides some of the Joyces' food and a great deal of their heating. The living room is the central room of the house with its books, its fireplace—cheerful on chilly desert nights— and the built-in banquettes that are lined with pillows and invite relaxing. It is a room that gives a sense that laughter is often shared under its beams, and earnest conversations before the fire.

This is a house that uses every inch of its capacity thoughtfully and well. Every element of this cool, quiet house has been carefully chosen to give comfort, pleasure, and sustenance, and to protect and enlarge the lives being lived there.

Living Room

The living room is centered on the corner fireplace, which is flanked by built-in banquettes lined with pillows the couple had made from remnants of nine-teenth-century Appalachian weaving. The rocker in the foreground is an example of the American Arts and Crafts style. The bench, doubling as a coffee table, belonged to Tom's grandfather, a sign painter. Tom made the iron candle-chandelier, the fire tongs, and a number of other pieces around the room. Built-in pedestals framing the banquettes serve as end tables and define seating and space. On the bookshelf near the fireplace is a branch from a cork-screw willow the couple planted on the property. The door at the rear of the room leads to the Joyce girls' living quarters.

Detail

A folded raffia skirt from Africa hangs in one corner of the living room. On the adjoining wall is a collage made of phone books from East and West Germany by Helmut Lohr, a German artist with whom Tom collaborated. On the tabletop beneath the raffia skirt is a forged bowl, an African sculpture of mother and child, and a bronze miniature of a phytosaur by Tom's friend Phil Bircheff. Tom and Phil have excavated fossil remains together, and on one dig discovered the four-foot-long fossil head of a phytosaur. Paleontology is one of Tom's interests.

Living Room, Detail   l e f t

On another wall, a collection of African art includes a sodden carved granary door depicting blacksmithing. The carving on the tabletop is of a small ax designed to carve masks. Tom enjoys investigating other cultures through their art and artifacts.

Living Room, Detail   r i g h t

Stairs lead from the living room up to the master bedroom. Tom made all the stair rails in the house. A wooden pattern for casting and a pair of tar birds (paper with tar over them) by John Connell sit at the foot of the ceramic sculpture, by Gretchen Wach, on the upper pedestal. On the floor, at left, is a Santo Domingo bear-claw pot. On the baseboard, resting against the lower pedestal, is a piece of slate carved by Tom's father, whose hobby was carving. On the floor nearby is a fragment from a sixteenth-century English limestone column given to Tom by a man he had just met and with whom he formed an instant friendship. The little iron ball on the corner of the lower pedestal is what's left of a coyote trap that Julie found — with a coyote caught in it. She freed the coyote, and Tom melted down the trap and hammered it into a small ball so that it could never again catch a wild animal.

146

Drafting Studio   l e f t

Hanging or lying all around the desk are prototypes of projects, from a wall sconce to gates and balcony railings. Tom makes prototypes for clients and architects who want to see the three-dimensional aspects of the project. Meanwhile, he gets some practice in executing the commission. The framed photograph propped against the wall is of a gate that was a commission for the former residence of artist Georgia O'Keeffe.

Forge, Detail   b e l o w

Found objects on a table in the corner of the forge are being assembled into floor and table lamps for Tom's house. In the window is a metal player-piano disk that will be made into a lampshade.

Kitchen   l e f t

Tom designed much of the house's woodwork and cabinetry, which was built by a local carpenter, C. J. Martin, who became a friend. The kitchen floor is buff Arizona flagstone set in cement. The same flagstone covers the floor of the greenhouse, but is set there in sand. Structolite plaster is used in the walls of the kitchen and living room. The door and window lead to the greenhouse, which is on the same level, and to the herb beds just outside. Tom learned to make wheel-thrown pottery years ago and made many dishes for the family's use.

Bedroom

The walls are covered in mud plaster. The floors here and elsewhere in the house are fir. The quilt on the bed was found at a local crafts fair. The banjo at the foot of the bed is not just a decoration—playing the banjo is another one of Tom's achievements. The Navajo rug on the floor represents a teaching project in which an older woman teaches a younger one. The increasing mastery of the weaving technique can actually be seen across the rug and provides a history of the learning process. The idea delights Tom, who likes to use the things he collects aesthetically and as collections for study. The iron bowl on the tabletop in the left foreground is one of Tom's "scrap" bowls. The tall wooden structure leaning against the closet wall in the background is an African ladder. Under the desk beneath the window is the opening that allows the air to rise from the greenhouse and return when it has become cooled.

Exterior　At sunset, the Joyces' house is bathed in the exquisite Santa Fe light.

The work of and information about the craftsmen featured in this book can be found at the following galleries:

ALAN BROWN *Tommy Simpson, Missy Stevens*	Hartsdale, NY (914) 686-3900	LEW ALLEN CONTEMPORARY ART *Tom Joyce, Missy Stevens*	129 West Palace Ave. Santa Fe, NM 87510 (505) 988-8997
THE ART COLLECTOR *Nancy Jurs*	4151 Taylor St. San Diego, CA 92110 (619) 299-3232	MARK MILLIKEN GALLERY *Thomas Mann*	1200 Madison Ave. New York, NY 10128 (212) 534-8802
BARRY FRIEDMAN LIMITED *Bennett Bean*	32 East 67th St. New York, NY 10021 (212) 794-8950	MARTHA CONNELL GALLERY *Sam Maloof, Leo Sewell*	333 Buckhead Atlanta, GA 30305 (404) 261-1717
BRYAN OHNO GALLERY *Wendell Castle*	15 South Main St. Seattle, WA 98104 (206) 667-9572	MAURINE LITTLETON GALLERY *Albert Paley*	1667 Wisconsin Ave. NW Washington, DC 20007 (202) 333-9307
CLARK GALLERY *Leo Sewell, Tommy Simpson*	P.O. Box 339 Lincoln Station Lincoln, MA 01773 (781) 259-8303	NANCY SACHS GALLERY *Dave and Roberta Williamson*	7700 Forsyth St. Louis, MO 63105 (314) 727-7770
DEL MANO GALLERY *Sam Maloof*	1981 San Vincente Blvd. West Los Angeles, CA 90049 (310) 476-8508	PETER BARTLOW GALLERY *Nancy Jurs*	44 East Superior Chicago, IL 60611 (312) 337-1782
DIANE KEMPLER/STUDIO *Diane Kempler*	675 Drewry St. Atlanta, GA 30306 (404) 892-0522	PRITAM AND EAMES *James Schriber*	29 Race Lane Easthampton, NY 11937 (516) 324-7111
DONAHUE GALLERY *Lenore Tawney*	560 Broadway, No. 304 New York, NY 10012 (212) 226-1111	R. DUANE REED GALLERY *Bennett Bean, Wendell Castle*	No. 1 North Taylor at LaClede St. Louis, MO 63108 (314) 361-8872
FERRIN GALLERY *Thomas Mann, Roy and Mara Superior*	179 Main St. Northampton, MA 01060 (413) 586-4509	RICHARD MAFONG STUDIO *Richard Mafong*	875 Piedmont NE Atlanta, GA 30309 (404) 881-9847
FREEHAND GALLERY *Dave and Roberta Williamson*	8413 West 3rd St. Los Angeles, CA 90048 (213) 655-2607	RILEY HAWK GALLERIES *Wendell Castle*	2026 Murray Hill Road Cleveland, OH 44106 (216) 421-1445
GALLERY NAGA *Tommy Simpson*	67 Newbury St. Boston, MA 02116 (617) 267-9060	RIVA YARES GALLERY *Albert Paley*	3625 Bishop Lane Scottsdale, AZ 85251 (602) 947-3251
HAND & SPIRIT GALLERY *Thomas Mann, Tommy Simpson*	4222 North Marshall Way Scottsdale, AZ 85251 (602) 946-4529	SAM MALOOF STUDIO *Sam Maloof*	9553 Highland Ave. P.O. Box 51 Al Paloma, CA 91701
HIBBERD-MCGRATH GALLERY *Missy Stevens*	101 North Main St. Breckenridge, CO 80424 (970) 453-6391	SNYDERMAN GALLERY *Roy Superior*	303 Cherry St. Philadelphia, PA 19106 (215) 238-9576
JOHN ELDER GALLERY *Nancy Jurs, James Schriber*	529 West 20th St. New York, NY 10011 (212) 462-2600	THOMAS MANN GALLERY *Thomas Mann*	1804 Magazine St. New Orleans, LA 70130 (504) 581-2113
JON ERIC RIIS DESIGN LTD. *Jon Eric Riis*	875 Piedmont NE Atlanta, GA 30309 (404) 881-9847	TWIST N.W. *Thomas Mann*	30 NW 23rd Place Portland, OR 97210 (503) 224-0334
LEO KAPLAN MODERN *Wendell Castle, Albert Paley Tommy Simpson, Missy Stevens*	41 East 57th St., 7th Floor New York, NY 10022 (212) 535-2407	THE WORKS GALLERY *Leo Sewell, Missy Stevens, Mara Superior, Dave and Roberta Williamson*	303 Cherry St. Philadelphia, PA 19106 (215) 922-7775